Shattered Shame
& Rejection

Uncovering the Modern Day Molech

(Nabiha Kelly)

ISBN (978-0-692-94913-9)

Printed in USA by 48HrBooks (www.48HrBooks.com)

Dedication

In loving memory,
of my favorite Aunt Carla Melissa Kelly.
I would like to dedicate this book to you,
because you were the one there for me many times
while I was growing up.

Acknowledgements

If it had not been for the Lord on my side, where would I be? In life, we encounter many people on the journey. Some people come and go, and then there are others who like pillars remain planted in our life. This book would not have come to fruition without the support and encouragement of crucial persons along the way. The writing process for this book was not without difficulty and challenges; however, it is the contribution of key persons whose help brought this piece of literary work orchestrated by God to life. Father, I thank you for giving me your Son Jesus Christ and your precious Holy Spirit. It has and continues to be one of the most meaningful relationships in my life. Serving you Lord has been nothing short of the best in life, and I thank you for allowing me to be Nabiha. I am one with faults, frailties, gifting, and abilities that can only come from a loving Dad like you. To my favorite *Aunt Carla Melissa Kelly*. I often think about how life would be now if you were still around. I reminisce on the days when you and *Uncle Dale Kelly* took turns picking me up from nursery and primary school. Even though I would cry all the time, you both knew how to trick me into being quiet with some 'Now & Later' candy. I miss you very much and may you sleep in peace, my dear Aunt. Thank you, *Mom* for being such a hard-working woman. As a single mother, you provided and gave your very best. To my sister *Renita-Jo*, you have always been there for me through many trials and triumphs. To my favorite cousin *Selena*, through thick and thin you are always there. You have never judged me, and the book you are witnessing will be the splendor of God's hand in my life. Thank you to the *Kelly Family*, my late grandfather *Colwin Kelly*, and a vast amount of cousins and extended family.

The bible states that he who wins souls is wise, and *Stephanie Stephenson*, my dear friend, and sister, may your crown in heaven be great as God used you to be the vessel that would lead me to Him; I love you. To my spiritual mother *'Gretchi' Maudriana Grant*, you know me in and out. Thank you for your endless intercession for me. To the Demolition Crew, my prayer partners of 365 days of each year, *Liza Johnson* and *Anita Pedroza-Walcott*, thank you. To the 'Dream Team'. *Daniella Francis, Dr. Nathan Culver* and *Raimon Norris*. Thank you for allowing me the time to get comfortable with my story. A huge thanks to my professors at the Nyack College-Alliance Theological Seminary Doctoral program, *Dr. Martin Sanders* and *Dr. Rob Reimer*. To my former colleagues at *St. Dominics Home Family*, you all played an integral part in my journey.

Confidants are a rare and most treasured commodity. *Cherlyn Carby*, you fit the whole essence of what a true confidant looks and feels like, thank you for loving, listening, and being that objective voice in my life. You are greatly appreciated. To my *Bishop Rowan J. Edwards*, thank you for always believing in me and seeing the destiny set out by God. Thank you, *Neil.* We have been through so much and had a lot of history together. This book would not be possible without your endless and selfless sacrifices each day. You always provided for the family, and I thank you sincerely. To my two beautiful children *Demetrius* and *Hannah*, wow is all I can say. There are many lessons that I have learned as a parent. You both are precious and powerful gifts given to me by God and can and will accomplish all you are faced with in life. *Demetrius* this book will make history, as I have seen the hand of God on your life from day one. Tears always fill my eyes when I think about the goodness and forgiveness of God, as we both have been through countless storms. Son, you have proven that the Devil has no power over our lives, and the best is yet to come. I love you, Meech! *Hannah,* you are the best princess any mother could receive from

God. When I was pregnant with you, I miscarried, but God supernaturally brought you back. Indeed you are a special child, and God has an excellent work for you to do. I cover you both, my children, under the blood of Jesus. When the enemy sees the blood of Jesus, he has no choice but to pass over!

Table of Contents

Preface i

Introduction 1

Part I: Room #1 5

Chapter 1 Life is a Road! 5

Chapter 2 There is no Good Thing in the Flesh! 16

Chapter 3 GO Home; Come Forth 27

Chapter 4 Paroled: 7-time Felon 41

Part 2: Room #2 53

Processed in the Dark Room 53

Chapter 5 My Vow, 1999 57

Chapter 6 Dead End: Death and Life, 2001 66

Chapter 7 Come to a prayer meeting, 'it' will change your life 76

Chapter 8 The Shame is Over! 108

Chapter 9 You will be a sacrifice, 2018 127

About the Author 140

Preface

Photograph of Molech. *Christian Image Source*, christianimagesource.com

Leviticus 18:21 KJV- *And thou shalt not let any of thy seed pass through the fire of Molech, neither shalt thou profane the name of thy God: I am the Lord.*

2 Kings 23:10 KJV- *And he defiled Topheth, which is in the valley of the children of Hinnom, that no man might make his son or his daughter to pass through the fire to Molech.*

Molech is the biblical name of a Canaanite god associated with child sacrifice. The name of this deity is also referred to as Moloch, Milcom, or Malcam. Molech is the god of child sacrifice. He was an Old Testament false god that children were given over to be sacrificed. These particular sacrifices resulted in being placed in a area called Topheth. Topheth meant 'place of burning' or 'place of fire'. It was at this site where the people of Israel worshiped Molech. The primitive root word 'toph' means playing or beating a percussion instrument. Instruments such as a timbre, tambourine, or drum were used during these ceremonies. IT was believed that the noise from the percussion instruments would drown out the sounds of infants as they were passed through the fire and burned alive. Much is hidden concerning Molech, however, as a Prophetess of God, I come as a voice with the platforms given to demolish these alters so that lives can be free, liberated, catapulted and launched in their destiny.

Introduction

Shattered Shame & Rejection Uncovering the Modern Day Molech, is a book impressed and inspired back in 2002. The Holy Spirit whispered to me that this book would be used to unveil the repercussions of abortion and all of its deficits, hurt, lies, and deceit. As I pondered on how this book should be written, it is and has been the most challenging writing process because it deals with being wholly transparent so others will be set free. However, I begged to know, why Lord? Why can't someone else take this task? I knew so many that could fit the part; nevertheless, I came to the realization I would not be relieved of this. As this is a part of the ministry, the Lord has graced to me. The transformation, restoration, and deliverance of lives are what the Lord told me would take place. This book is by far, one of the most complicated, and in a sense taboo for too many in Christian churches, around the globe and within our local communities. This manuscript will be used as a tool to invade various cultures for those who have been bound by religion and legalism. Jesus' purpose on earth was to reconcile man to God and to tear down and destroy the works of the devil. Molech! This spirit consistently plagues many generations of people, and within these pages in this opportune season, its release is imminent and conducive to the setting free of its captives.

If you have ever felt hurt, rejection, shame, condemnation, or do not feel deserving of the Fathers love, then this book will be a kaleidoscope to your breakthrough. Whether you are a man, woman, young girl or boy, this book will change your life. The criticism and the judgment that may follow, Lord have your way. May our eyes be enlightened through the eyes of faith, as there is hope for all who believe. On these pages to follow, this book can also be used as a tool to help the deteriorating generation we see every day going astray. Speaking on this topic in youth groups, women conferences, and men fellowship can and will bring empowerment while shedding insight. For where the Spirit of God is there is liberty, and the truth will set you free. Our youth need guidance, and it is the time for faithful men and women of God who will stand up in the face of the adversary, to educate and impart wisdom and direction to those in need. The Bible clearly states that elders must be in a place to teach the younger; but if the elders are not equipped, then the cycle will continue. We adjure that leaders of our nation and churches will not be the only individuals who are populating heaven but will grab those on the descending steps to hell.

As you read this book I implore, urge, and beckon that you just not read this book as the next novel and put it down. I am asking that you read and digest this book as you reflect on your own life, as well as others who you believe may be in need of a reprieve. Let there be a revolt in your spirit to cry aloud and spare not, to those that come from vastly dysfunctional homes with evident depravity in our family unit. There is a purpose in doing our part in saving others. So put on your seatbelts and be patient, loving and kind as the King of Glory will minister to you in ways you would never imagine. I invite you into the bedchamber of this writer so that you will know the exact reason why God called, sanctioned, ordained and handpicked Prophetess Nabiha Kelly, a modern day Esther, for such a time as this to unveil herself uniquely and delicately. It is observed that when a person enters a house, there are various rooms. This book will take you into rooms in each section, for you to understand the compartments of my life, and a timeline of how my life changed. You will also see this writer as a friend and one who has laid her life down so that others will be free. I pray that your life will never be the same, that the love of the Father will fill your hearts and that healing will be your portion, as there is room at the foot of the cross. May you cast your cares upon him, for he cares for you and He paid the ultimate price for you and me to be saved, redeemed, and reconciled to the Glory of God. Plagues kill, but when the enemy sees the Blood of Jesus Christ he must PASSOVER!

Part I: Room #1

Chapter 1
Life is a Road!

It was a cold December night, in 1993, when I first felt as if an arrow was pointed in my direction. Of course, I do not mean in the literal sense, but in the bombshell of having gotten pregnant. How could I have let this happen at the age of fifteen? I have often heard about girls my age who were in my place, but I always said that could never be me. In much despair, I found myself at the Atlantic Avenue train station in Brooklyn, NY with a friend. At this time, I faced a significant life-altering decision whether to go through with such a horrible thing. Abortion never crossed my mind until the two of us spoke, as we were both in the same boat, however, she was much further along in her pregnancy. We sat there and talked, as both of us were in need of clarity. It felt like we were the blind leading the blind. We began to counsel one another in fear and desperation, discussing what should be our next move. We realized that so many of our peers faced or underwent what we were currently going through, in their own lives. Our 'parents' would kill us or better yet, it would ruin their Caribbean upbringing to have their daughters bring this shame on the family. "How absurd," I thought. At that moment, I made my decision, as I was not taught about sex. Instead, I was urged to finish school, get good grades, be obedient to my elders, and DON'T GET PREGNANT.

During this time, the internet was not as widely used as it is today, but to my surprise, a vast amount of literature on abortion was readily available for underage young girls. To my surprise, I saw how accessible this process was to each person in pursuit of this option. However, not surprising, abortion was an element used by many, especially girls who did not want anyone to find out. What I find striking, is approval to have an abortion did not require consent from a caregiver, however, to obtain a driver's permit, state identification, or a license a parent must be present. All an individual needed to do was pay $300-400 or get government insurance, and all can be done sweat less or hurriedly. Pro-Choice, what is that, if all the options you have at a tender age are billboard advertisements or the yellow pages that indicate it could be done, two, and three. With much anxiety, I was guided in this process without even consulting with an adult. I hid and stopped dressing in front of my mother. I would put on the garment of lies and deceit. I thought to myself, was this how it was supposed to happen? Is this the way and is it safe and much less is it right? As thoughts flooded my mind, I was in a confused and afraid state; the reign of my mind was a battleground. I began to daydream that my mother would never find out because if she did, the whole family would know. It would be a horrid thing for them to understand, as they would view me as a disgrace. I grew up in a single parent home with little to no supervision; there was not much of a role model or person available to talk to me about the birds and the bees. I felt the saying was foolishness, as there is no such thing as insects cuddling. It was a young girl on the road to a place of no return. I was in a place where I drifted so far and was not sure how I made it out alive. It was a time of destitution where I had feelings of hopelessness and shame. I did not want this thing to happen to me; I was ashamed and embarrassed. I felt extraordinarily disgust and disappointment in myself to have allowed my internally classified careless behavior to manifest in such an outward thing.

Looking in the mirror, I can honestly say that I did not know the person in the reflection. I was at rock bottom, attempting to learn the process of how to 'get rid of' my issue! I heard the best time to have an abortion was between 8-12 weeks. Therefore, to add to my high emotions, the waiting process seemed to be a longer death sentence that taunted me and probed at my psyche. I did not want to feel. I was out of touch with the young woman who was looking back in the mirror. I thought that if this procedure is so great, why the wait? The answer was the abortionist had to make sure that the baby was developing so as there would not be any possibility of residue or perhaps baby parts remaining. Ugh, how could they be so graphic of something that was so easy? It all hit me at once, and I was being set up to pursue a road that was deep and wide. A road that was winding and treacherous. To my surprise, so many young girls were more than three months pregnant, which meant they had to have a completely different procedure as opposed to the ones in an earlier phase. You see my friend there are various methods of abortions. Some that are supposed to be less invasive, and less traumatic. Really! I mean these young women were carrying three, four and five-month-old babies inside their wombs. Some of their stomachs were so small no one would ever think this person was with child. This practice was the death penalty! What is going on? They made a vow to participate in the lethal saline injection, which is a solution, injected gradually causing uterine contractions, as if you are in a place to give birth. People who wait a more extended period in their pregnancy push out this pseudo birth, designed to kill the fetus or embryo.

On the other hand, I felt as if I was a saint and my procedure was not as bad, but it was only a trick of the enemy. I believed that my time would not be as gruesome, but dumb in a sense to think that Satan plays fair. He does not! I was behooved, set up and propelled to move forward, tagged as being the most wanted murderer. A covering cast or veil was on my eyes as I walked down to the slaughterhouse. Desperate, I was crying within hoping that the day would go by fast, never to return. I was too ashamed to turn back or let an adult know. I was an 'A' student, cheerleader, and involved in so many activities at school. I even was graduating from high school a whole year early. All I knew at this particular time was I have to keep this a secret. I hung out with friends who also were in the same position and needed the guidance of a mother or a mature nurturing embrace. I had to toughen up, square my shoulders and proceed with blinders on my eyes so that I would not see the picketers outside. They held up still pictures of aborted fetuses while screaming and shouting. They even began pulling on me and calling me a murderer. There were nuns and the whole rosary team in attendance deeming me to hell, and I still went ahead to advance the kingdom of hell by doing the unpardonable. Murderer, murderer, murderer! It still rings in my ears, as it was a mental photograph taken that when I revert to this experience; all I can remember are those words.

Numb, with moments of isolated tears, I was in need of a comforting voice to convey that everything would be okay. No one spoke those words, instead I was given gestures of encouragement to sign on the dotted line of consent, to see a counselor, undress, and put on the surgical robe. The front and back were tied, and a blue meshed shower cap covered my hair. Nabiha Kelly your number has been called you are next in line. This was not a call for Miss America or valedictorian, but a call to be a part of the chosen ones used as a vessel, to be used in the murder to an add-on in worshipping Molech. This murder did not require a handgun, or a switchblade, all it required was a pretty caramel young girl, now a lost sheep with scales on her eyes headed on a journey that would land her in many pit stops to hell.

I can still smell that eerie day, the alcohol swabs, and the smell of metal as the bright surgical lights shined above my head. I had the option of going to sleep or being awake, and actually, I thought being awake would have been better, but I should have been prepping for the morgue. The room felt like a crime scene and was cold and drab. I could hear the nurse and the anonymous doctor converse saying, "Here goes another one." Boy! Were they talking about me as if I were not even there? I am not chopped liver! They did not care, and I was just another one that bit the dust. An ordinary misinformed girl with much despair and trauma happening all at the same time.

The abortionist, I mean the doctor, seemed so comfortable in doing this ritual thing. He and the nurse probably had so many notches under their belt. There have been so many thoughts and suppressed sadness regarding the choice I was about to make. As I relive this part of my life, the same feeling I had when entering the room, still feels evident and surreal today. All I can hear is, "Nabiha scoot down to the edge of the table; open wide and relax, I am just going to numb you a bit on each side of your cervix" as if I were not already there. I could hear my heartbeat and feel my right eye filled with endless tears flowing down my face. Horrified, devastated, and confused, thoughts of being the most stupid girl in the world. The dirtiest person alive on earth and the worst human being.

When I observed the prep room, there were many surgical instruments, and a jar positioned next to them.

My narrow ankles were propped in the gray stirrups, and a metal speculum inserted to medicate each side of my cervical area. The pain intensified as the long needle was applied, squirt and squirt. I can feel the inside of my thighs go dead and heavy as a loud vacuum sound permeated the atmosphere. As the inserted plastic tip entered, the suction began to make an awful noise. The feeling of the tugging and pulling and then the closing of a jar and the words 'it's all out'. The curet, a sharp object used during this procedure, was scraping and pruning all particles out. It is incredible that my whole womb and uterine walls were not ripped away by the force that seemed to be higher than a Hoover vacuum used in homes. Then in motion, and being pulled into the recovery room, I thought this was the worst but most relieving day of my life. Afterward, they gave me warm tea and saltine crackers with peanut butter for nourishment. Once I was awake, all I could think of is its time to move on. Plotting what my next move would be once I left this dreadful place.

As I left the room where the procedure took place, I could see all eyes staring, laughing, jesting, and slightly darting at me. Especially the ex-embryo's father, my counterpart who was looking confused and dumbfounded. Also present was a so-called friend, who I later found out wanted the father. She ended up dating him, but that is a whole other story. All I cared to do was go to cheerleading practice and put this entire episode behind me. I came to the realization that a spirit had taken hold of me the moment I laid on the table and gateways were open. Portals and access ways that flooded my body. It was a spirit or darkness hovering over me for many days or rather years to come. I had traded places with the devil, and he was the puppeteer while finagling me on the strings.

The spirit Molech also referred to as Malchon, Ashtoreth, or Baal were all false gods, which many went after in the days of the Old Testament. Molech was the god that was worshipped and known to those who wanted to perform a child sacrifice or modern day terms abortion. In I Kings 11 Solomon traded places with serving the God of Israel and went after strange women and their gods. This was an abomination in the eyes of the God of Israel. I, too, had committed various abominable things and never in a million years did I consider myself a murderer. Understand, the day I went to have the procedure I picked up many things but left my soul behind. I often found myself drifting and wondering would I have the ability to feel again, or would I ever get that youthful glow back. Frankly, the glow was tainted by various contributing factors that all fall under the umbrella of murder. Murder is a strongman, a stronghold, and if the strongman is not torn down, it will grow stronger, picking up momentum like a hurricane or any natural disaster for that matter.

The Spirit of Molech is not something one desires to pursue, but when I found myself in that place, I could feel the missiles piercing and coming so strong. I was open to the world of promiscuity, lude living, reckless behavior and just being a product of hurt, lost girl trying to find herself and not been able to be seen. I walked in the works of the flesh, and I did not care about anyone, not even myself anymore. In Galatians 5:19-21 states: "Now the works of the flesh are manifest, which are these; Adultery, fornication, uncleanness, lasciviousness, Idolatry, witchcraft, hatred, variance, emulations, wrath, strife, seditions, heresies, envying's, murders, drunkenness, reviling's, and such like: of the which I tell you before, as I have also told you in time past, that they which do such things shall not inherit the kingdom of God."

There is power of life and death in the words that we speak. This spirit was spoken over my life while I was in my mother's womb. Family members made suggestions to my mom that she should have an abortion. They would consider me an untimely child born out of wedlock. How could someone want an innocent child killed in the womb? This spirit followed me for so many years; Molech had captivated me and had possessed my very existence. I felt conditioned to the time in which I lived. I gained strength from whatever demon was thrusting me into entanglement. The war was real, and forces of darkness had taken dominion in my life. Whatever road I chose, I met with distractions and hindrances on the way to my predestined destiny. The path I chose had many fractures because of the many roads traveled on. It led to significant setbacks and much heartache. The broad road is destructive. The road less traveled there are benefits. There are many hiccups along life's journey.

Chapter 2

There is no Good Thing in the Flesh!

As the black widow spider is weaving her web, I was nestled as a prey in the nucleus, once Molech had put his mark on my head. A seed was planted. Broad is the road to destruction as promiscuity was the vehicle I drove. I sanctioned and became a candidate running for the most men to sleep with. I began to open doors that I never knew existed. These doors did not grant me access to blessings and opportunity. They were doors that afforded me with wrenching things that one could endure. Different men on top of my body and at times I would never use protection. I was not immune to contracting sexually transmitted diseases. To think HIV, syphilis, gonorrhea, herpes, amongst many more, and God protected me. It was God there all those times when I was in the gutter. It was in the silent moments I prayed God please have mercy on me, I have a good heart. I am just hurting and in need of love. I talked to God during my areas of faultiness and knew that internally I had so many conditions in need of attention. My heart condition was very hard similar to concrete. It was hard from the walls and barriers of pain I did not want to feel. I was not a person who wanted others to feel pain, but most of my hurt was self-inflicted. It was hurt I endured because I could not forgive myself. It was hurt and pain deposited inside of me, and I was not warranted the opportunity to feel again.

There is a saying that we all have skeletons that are in the back of our closets, but the truth is do we have skeletons or is it a graveyard? I was a grave carrier. I was offered up as a sacrifice, which it perpetuated time again by the grips of the forces of darkness chaining me to the extremities of this bitter and cruel world. The love of money became my god. Nice cars driven by men who had influence and money was my desire. My mind was on traveling to lavish places but in reality, I was on a treadmill going nowhere. A girl with a pretty face, but a fractured character, tainted past, and I was a partaker in the devices of destroying my generation further. I attracted all types of things, but strange spirits continued to follow me. I was a good person making poor decisions, which would affect my very existence. Sex was a free gift, or should I say it was not free. I walked in the role of a high-class prostitute, never having to enter a brothel. I did not have to walk on a strip or have a pimp to control me. It was all behind the closed doors of endless mattresses, cars, or wherever. The moment I gave your body over to another person and money was placed on a hotel nightstand, I had accomplished my goal. I would use the money to purchase of clothes, shoes, and handbags. I never considered myself as a call girl or a prostitute, but I was a good registrant. You see I had an incredible gift of influence. The influence I carried was that I could captivate anything or anyone. It would be a tool I used to obtain the things I desired by manipulation and control. I was confident that I could step into any arena and command the attention without saying one word. I could see whom these individuals were, those who held power and were top of the line in business or the drug game and could get anything from them. I felt there was no time to love or to foster a relationship so from testosterone to testosterone I prevailed.

I can honestly say I have never been open to same-sex relationships nor did I have a desire to entertain such relationships. With a captivating personality, I had the gift for luring and capturing men into my web, and once they wanted commitment, I would spew them out with the venom of a nonchalant response. I was a runner. I rejected many and felt undeserving of ever wishing to embrace feelings of intimacy ever again. I felt that if I would allow my heart to be entangled that my counterparts would have gotten the best of me. I felt to love or be in love was for weak people. The truth of the matter is I was a coward who ran and was running a losing race. What was love anyway? Who was worth me loving them or receiving their love? Love was a forbidden variable! This race caused much despair and tragedy, and by the time I walked out of high school, I was a walking sepulcher. I would attend many parties, but I was never into drinking alcohol. I partied seven days a week, attending industry parties, events and things that portrayed the glamorous life. In hindsight, I know now that I have an impulsive and addictive personality, as there was no medium or balance. I was a very reactive person and if the wind blew me, I was there. There was no anchorage in my soul; I was carefree and free of really taking life seriously. It led me from one extreme situation to the other. I am grateful to have never dibbled and dabbled in any illicit drugs like cocaine, crack or alcohol because if I did, I would not have made it to write this book. I remember someone said to me that I was as a drug, and anyone who got a taste, figuratively or literally would become an addict.

Addictions, if not careful can kill and weaken any prey. Our addictions can propel us down pathways that requires deliverance on a greater level. Our addictions reveal how much we truly know ourselves. When we are led by our own addictions, it can send us on a wild goose chase always searching to be high, and once that high is not reached, we begin to incorporate it with other things. It can appear that there is no satisfaction in life, no satisfaction in the simple things. You often find yourself gambling with life and taking risks that can propel you over the edge. My addictions were a clear indication that I needed something. I also found out that friends or foes were my catalysts to my addictions. I had many 'frenemies', people pretending to be my friends, but they were enemies, thieves, liars, and haters. Their thoughts and opinions never mattered because when you are not conscious or self-aware, you keep on operating with the same behavioral default patterns. The cycles repeat and to you end up finding out that much was missed when you awaken from your spiritual slumber.

I was high off the spirit that was carrying me. I could feel the density of the cloud hovering over me everywhere I would go. This cloud was so dark that it concealed the real me. When I think of the mercy and grace of God, I become teary. I roll back the curtains of my remembrance and see the protection of HIS blood. That even in the grips of hells gate, HIS hand was there waiting to save. In addition, assessing all that I have been through it was quite nerve wrecking that I could have contracted sexually transmitted diseases that I could not get rid of. I would take many HIV tests and be so afraid, but once my test reported I was negative, I continued on my rampage. In all honesty, I was in search of that thing or wanted to recapture the moment I allowed a man ever to touch me with a loving embrace. I never found it but gained baggage and depths of the scent of men that would not go away. I could smell the men and their chemistry on me, a walking apothecary with a stench that was from the gutter. I could smell the colognes, the semen, and the odors of the different men when I showered or used the bathroom. The more I showered, the more I could smell and crave certain scents. The scents were an indication of my ties to each sexual counterpart. I would use vaginal cleansers such as Norforms vaginal suppositories, Summer's Eve Douches, and more but still it would not flush away any of those smells. Those smells were indicative that a man still resided in my body, that there were many soul ties attached to me, which is why I could not break free from walking in my flesh. My prey was not in the web; I was tangled up in the yoke of bondage. I would know that the soul ties were present, because I would go to certain places such as clubs, lounges, hotels, restaurants, basketball games, shows, beaches, etc., and the scents would protrude my nostrils. They triggered a memory that would have me either call or meet up with whichever soul tie I had in mind. Once the connection took place, I would meet with them and once it was over, I was back on a mission with no remorse or shamefacedness. I embodied a huge boldness of a lioness on a prowl.

I pretended to look well and be happy, acting normal, but my world was crumbling and the pieces were all on the floor. So many persons had trampled my life getting what they wanted and discarding me. Then again, was it the same on my part? My beautiful heart was broken. I had a heart that could not feel. It did not hurt, as I allowed the masses to break me down to pieces. False friends sold me short and gave me over to behaviors that were not permitted correction. Laughter and so-called friends who said they loved me, and would call me their girl would later find out they too were like passing ships in a sultry ocean tossing to and fro. Many of those unfriendly friends were jealous and envious of me, as they too desired the men in my life. They wanted to live vicariously through my life, but who would want filth of another person? However, many heard about my past encounter with Molech, and it was a topic for many discussions. They all wanted to see me head down a road of no return. Many of them had the shovels in their hand and the hammer to nail the coffin shut. In retrospect, growing up without a parent who knew nothing about life on the streets and no father present, my idea of relationships did not mean much. I never heard the words I love you. I only saw heartless marriages crumble. I did not witness any level of intimacy between a man and woman. I never knew how to love, and the way I did was to give my body as a token to feel some warmth or affection. At the tender age of six, I experienced rejection. This rejection was the driving force to not experiencing true love because of the vows I made to myself. I can recall in my childhood memories of a man who showed and displayed much affection for me. The thought that pictures are worth a thousand words seem to be right. In recent years, things became more apparent to me. I sat one day in my doctoral class, listening to my professor speak. He later turned and said in front of my colleagues "Nabiha, your issue is not spiritual, its emotional deprivation, and I am recommending you see someone who is excellent on inner and emotional healing." I then realized that there were areas of my life that I experienced rejection and damage.

Rejection was another spirit thrown in with a monkey wrench that continued to follow me throughout life's journey. I felt that I never rejected anyone, but that was a lie. I rejected friends, family and even those genuine men who wanted a pure relationship with me. I was a runner. I felt that if I could hide my emotional sleeve, and make up an excuse or find something wrong with them, then that would be my way of escape from ever having to deal with sentimental things. Emotional scarring for me was always so closely linked to my rejection. During those moments of fear, things that came to remind me that I was not good enough and it caused me to withdraw further. This rejection, when it presented itself, would always remind me of the wounded girl at that very tender age who had been robbed of the essence of experiencing love. At the age of six, I found out who my biological father was. He was a kind man, but I learned very early that if a man promises you they are coming and never show up, then their promises do not mean anything. I can also recall as a young girl my biological father stating that he was going to pick me up. I waited out the 5th-floor window in Brooklyn hoping and praying he would show up. There was no call, no show! I developed that I would never wait for any man; I will do it myself and get whatever job done on my own. The attitude that developed caused me to lack respect in men and to become a woman who was self-reliant and self-sufficient, not depending any deadbeat father. What I received from my father was probably $2-$5 in total with two large punk rock safety pins and sparing birthday party appearance. I have longed forgiven my natural father after having an opportune time for us to sit and spend a weekend together. I found out he was the missing piece to the puzzle of the makeup of my personality. He was a kind and loving person, but he had a depth to his eyes as he looked at me. Moreover, rejection was the feeling sent to blind me on my journey.

Walking in the spirit of promiscuity caused me to have ideas of being an erotic dancer. I was determined as lust took over me and I was embraced with the grips of operating with another force. I was a drug addict to sex, and there was no quenching my sexual desires. The more I participated, the more I got deeper into the grip of the python. I often have to remind myself that I had to kill that sleeping giant {sexual urges}. I had to be careful not to wake up my desires from the past, as it was an addiction. Sex was the weapon I used, but so often sex was the knife I turned on myself repeatedly to continue engaging in these acts endlessly. When we can identify what has been holding us captive and the access points we have given over to the enemy, it is an opportune time to kill it from the root. To destroy the very thing which stands in the way of our destiny, the purpose of our life, the areas in which Satan continuously reminds us. The displaced shame and rejection we feel, causes us to doubt that we are God's choice and his child. A weapon used to silence voices that are contrary to what God has spoken to us from the beginning.   His word is sharp; it is quick, it brings everyone to the truth.

Chapter 3

GO Home; Come Forth

Hanging out with friends, working, and partying was the norm for a young woman. You did not have time to take things seriously, but there was much ambition. We graduated from high school and then moved onto college. To think we escaped the norm of becoming a teenage parent and dropping out of school. One day I was with a friend, and she took me with her to meet a guy she was dating at the time. He had a brother, and you know how the whole matchmaking thing goes. If you have a friend, then you hook them up with the brother and so on. If I had known the future, I would have been able to see what was about to happen, when I met this person. This hookup would lead to my demise. If only I had a father to protect me as his daughter and most prized possession, I know I would have made better choices in men. It was a short hook up, and one thing led to the other, and that April I got pregnant. I was only 18 years old and dating a significantly older man, in a relationship that was not mature. What would an older man want from this young woman? Toiling again, I thought to myself I might as well go back to the place I knew on the table.

On a chilly spring day, I decided to go to a different clinic because I knew there would be a different computer system, nurses, and doctors. No one would have heard my name or seen me before. Without hesitation, I dressed and did all the procedural things in preparation for 'surgery' again. Wait! This was no surgery! This is an abortion. I knew the process, so it was as if it was nothing to me. I knew all the ins and outs and seemed to be a pro at this. I was now in college and did not need any distractions. I wanted to continue with the party lifestyle, living the 'good' free life. In the pre-op room, a presence visited me and said, "leave and go home." What force was this? I never heard this audible voice before. Surely, I was not smoking marijuana {weed}; I was not hallucinating, or hearing strange voices. I never heard the voice of God, because all I knew was the god of the 'Catholic Priest'. I would take the first communion and say confession in the booth multiple times. Usually, when I make a decision, I never turn back. However, this time I began to shake and get nervous. The voice was not familiar. It was a thunderous voice; a voice that sounds an alarm when there is danger. At the time, I had already paid the money and was okay with moving forward, but this voice made me feel as if it was a ton of bricks placed on my legs, preventing me from stepping forward into the room. This voice was distinct, and there was a great nudging in my stomach, which made me feel very uneasy. Then there was an adamant jolt, a strong prompting, and I ended up canceling the procedure, leaving immediately. Dumbfounded, I wondered what was happening. I did not see anyone standing there telling me no, or was there anyone leading me out of the building. When I left, I felt relief and decided to continue with the pregnancy.

I can recall telling my mother I was pregnant, while she was on a trip with my grandmother. "Make sure you don't tell your grandmother while we are in Mexico," she said. As that would only make the trip come to an unexpected end. I was so embarrassed and felt that I let my family down. I told my mother I wanted to participate in having an abortion and she asked if she were to buy me shrimps from a restaurant formerly known as 'Crab Inn', would I reconsider and go through with the pregnancy. My grandmother eventually found out, "Nabiha what about contraception?" she said. Then the calls started pouring in. My uncle called and said I would complicate my life further. After that, my aunt called me wanting to set up an appointment to get rid of the baby. She kept saying I was too young. Even though

I was over the age of 18, they still saw me as a young girl. At that moment, I truly believed I was bringing shame to the family name. The shame of letting everyone down stayed on my mind. I thought of the shame that I would bring to their name by having a child out of wedlock. The truth is I already knew what silent shame felt like, as I hid the shame for many years. I covered the shame until part of my shame forced me to become performance-driven. I never wanted anyone to see this shame, so I masked it from people.

My relationships were very dysfunctional, but I was receiving attention in various ways. I found myself in a new culture, with persons who were hustlers. These were people far removed from what it takes to work in a structured working environment. Every other word coming out of their mouth was profanity, and their futures were not bright and deserving of success. Their family dynamic seemed loving, but the truth was they all were a product of their environment. They were friendly people, but it was apparent their upbringing was not all too good. They hung out late, drank, and did illicit activity. All of this occurring at the height of the crack era, when everywhere you turned someone was strung out on drugs. Strong depravity was visible in our communities; the role models were few, and those who had the rope chains, Versace shades, and flashy cars are what many chose to chase. I saw endless people who lost their way because of the use of drugs, trying to get a $5 hit. Prostitution was also rampant on the block I would frequent. I saw people selling drugs to their own family, and thinking to myself how absurd is this. These same people did not know what it was to have a job; their god was alcohol, profanity, significant levels of disrespect and more toward each other. I was a young girl entangled deeper in the grips of what was holding me captive, Molech.

Molech was gaining vigor, and its roots continued to get deeper. Even though I wanted a change, there was a lodging of another portal taking place. It felt like I was in quicksand and sinking quickly. In the delivery room, I was preparing to give birth. I remember my friend phoning the father and letting him know I was in labor. "Oh it's her first baby, she will be fine and there for a while," he said. His response crippled me, and he never showed up until later. This was my first experience giving birth, and it was a miserable and sad time. I thought that dating an older man would be different. That there would be a great level of excitement in knowing your baby is about to be born, but I was wrong. I began to weep as the missile of rejection launched and landed in my heart. Bulls-eye! Instantly something died in me, and I felt that level of rejection all over again.

Deep down, I knew that it was over between us. I would never feel the way I once did about him. Everything he would do turned me off, and I did not want to be with him anymore. I hated the sight and smell of him. The intimacy was off, and once I lost the baby weight and got back in shape, it was back on and popping. Puff Daddy and Biggie were popular artists at the time, and all I wanted to do was "F*** N*****, Get Money." I had no time for fake ones; I was about to bounce back and forget this whole idea of relationship and family. I was a young woman with a 'daddy syndrome', meaning a girl raised without a father. If not dealt with, one of the greatest wounds a child can experience throughout life is the wound from a mother or father. I was looking for an older man who would nurture, provide, protect and love me. He was none of the above, just very immature of life's realities. There was a severe void in my life.

Months after giving birth, I started to see a spirit of control and severe alcohol use. There were spurts of jealousy from the father, and I decided it was time to go. This started a whirlwind of contention, and he became verbally abusive. The disrespect of women was not something I saw growing up in my home. The men in my family were decent men, emotionally aloof, but professional and hard working. One day I was walking with friends on Flatbush Avenue, and we saw a booster, a term we used for someone who shoplifts. They were selling a beautiful Donna Karan dress, but the dress was too small for me as I was a top-heavy woman. I remember not wanting the dress triggered something in my son's father. He became physical with me in front of a friend and his family. This was a different person unfolding before my eyes. The demonstration of rage and anger displayed showed a great potential for extreme violence. I vividly remember him dragging me upstairs back into his apartment and kneeing me in my stomach, while I laid helpless on the couch. He had no idea I was pregnant at the time. Instantly, I began to hemorrhage, and I left the apartment and went home. I was having a spontaneous abortion, also known as a miscarriage. I would need to have a D&C. A dilation and curettage, also known as a D&C, is a surgical procedure often performed after a first-trimester miscarriage. It refers to opening the cervix and removing the contents of the uterus. Curettage is the scraping of the uterine wall with a curette instrument or by a suction curettage (also called vacuum aspiration). I never told the father about this pregnancy.

It was time to come up with a strategy to get out of this relationship. I started imagining myself being a young girl pushing a baby carriage, and not having my child's father around. Even though he did want to be in our lives, the relationship was toxic for me. There was a time when we lived together, and I came home later than usual from college. He began questioning and insulting me in front of his sister. He threw my clothes out in the hallway and said the baby was not his. He wanted me gone and called me all sorts of derogatory names. As his anger amplified, a fear came over me. I knew that I needed to protect my baby. That night I did not know whom to call, because I did not want to embarrass my family with this drama. Once again, I started feeling shame. The relationship only lasted for about a year and a half, and there was no emotional attachment to this man, so I called my aunt and asked her to come and get me. Our upbringing was different; I came from a single-family home full of strong women, and since I never experienced abuse in my house, I figured it would not be too hard to raise a young boy. I was fearless and knew that I had to act or something detrimental would happen. As we drove off, I never looked back. I had a drive and determination inside of me that I would make it without him. I had the confidence that I could grow a baby independently, but there was much resistance. There were never-ending calls, and he would show up at any given time stalking me at various places. He would come to my mother's home saying how he would hurt and kill me. I often tell others if you think you can walk in my shoes, I will gladly give them to you. Let us see how far you will reach in my size 8's. The aha moment is there is always a price to pay when a person takes care of you whether good or bad.

In New York City, the weather in November tends to be very chilly. On the night of November 13, 1997, I went back to my mother's house. I did not want to be a single mother depending on my mother for help. The next day, in a hopeless state, I took my baby and went on the #4 train. I was traveling to the Bronx to the EAU shelter, which is on 148th, and Grand Concourse for placement. I could never forget this time of my life, as I lifted the navy blue Kolcraft stroller up the stairs. This felt like devastation. Coming from a 'well to do' family, there was great humiliation, shame, and loneliness. I sat down in the shelter and watched as each person walked by me. When they called me for processing, reality hit me; I was about live amongst 'real' homeless people. I still proceeded to move forward with the process, trying to keep my head high. There was no time to chicken out; there was no other option. This shelter, a Tier II shelter, had a curfew. They made the decision to place me in another borough because I had an order of protection against the father. Which meant, I could not be present in the same borough the incident took place. The shelter placed me in Manhattan. I did not know anyone that lived in Manhattan, as all my family stayed in Brooklyn.

I traveled on the train from Manhattan to Brooklyn with a 10-month-old baby. I would leave at 4:30 am from the shelter, go to Brooklyn to drop the baby to the sitter and head back to Manhattan for work during the day and school at night. I was determined to graduate on time from college. During these times, I faced many life or death situations, which I can now see I went through for others coming.

Once I graduated from college, I was able to get a break for about five seconds. There was another component to face, having a son with challenges in school. I needed to find the appropriate setting for him. At the time he was only three years of age, and I remember picking him up from school in Brooklyn. I observed a teacher hitting him with a ruler and it left him with bruises on his arms. This incident led to legal proceedings and child protective services called against the school. Dealing with my son seemed to be a never-ending journey in securing the adequate help for him. He possessed so much strength for his age. He began to demonstrate severe oppositional and explosive behaviors. I was at times lost as to how I could find help for him. His first school provided me with information, suggesting that I should have him evaluated for special education. Evaluated? Special Education! I was so naïve in all of this. I thought to myself, what are these different evaluations? I heard terms like psychological help, psychiatric help, counseling and more. This was another component added to on this journey. Domestic violence, the evaluation process and my state of homelessness were all things to buffet my flesh. I felt like I was in a storm and there was no umbrella to shield me. I knew I had to bring this baby forth but did not know why as it was an intense struggle after struggle. The enemy kept saying if you would have aborted him you would not have had to deal with these challenges. I started to believe that I should have aborted my son. I began to develop a rejection in my heart toward him for all that I was going through while seeking help for him. I questioned why God would give me this particular baby. Knowing the seed he came from; I began to reject him inwardly because I felt he came to disrupt my life and make it uncomfortable. I felt like my life was a disaster because he was born. It took me back to the time a relative said that this baby would complicate my life. When my son began to have his episodes, it made me feel so helpless and enraged. Parenting became a very tedious chore. I forgot how to laugh, be free, and happy, all because of this baby. I had seen many people who were so delighted rearing children, but parenting for me was not a happy moment. I hated being a parent while others were rejoicing.

I was vexed, often blaming myself for things that were going wrong in my life. Why did I still have the numbness that I felt back at the age of 15? I began to decipher the importance of knowing the family history of the person you decide to have children with. We have to do our due diligence in finding out if there are generational curses, genetic diseases, mental health or unmet clinical needs. Things that can cause our lives to be interrupted or thrown off track. There are certain spirits assigned to hinder God's plan. I picked up a soul tie that sent to cause much deficit. Although my son has an even share of chromosomes from the both of us, he still has the equal share from his father. A moment of sexual pleasure can turn into a lifetime of bondage in a fruitless relationship. A broken relationship not built on the proper foundation can only deliver sex and the illusion of a fake orgasm, which is meaningless. Honestly, my son gained his father's genetic hard wiring. I never thought that after a relationship had ended that I would still deal with the ramifications of it. By this time, I was merely learning and trying to understand why these things were happening to me. It felt like a cosmic war was occurring. This war caused me to question if I should have canceled the abortion procedure that day. I have never really felt deep regrets until now.

Molech was still gripping the reins of my mind. I could feel the pull. Through much opposition and pain, I felt like life was unbearable at times. I became hesitant in wanting another child because of what I was going through raising this one. I felt in my heart that I should have killed him. I began to build barriers in my heart toward the behaviors my son started to exhibit. I dealt with his behavior and extreme demonic powers as they began to surface and present itself. My son's mental oppression and oppositional behavior were driving me further and further away from me wanting to be a parent. I had purposed in my heart that I would never have another child and that he was a child that came from the pit of hell. He began to manifest in demonic possession, and demonstrate one who was hearing from the underworld. How can this be? I come from a 'perfect' family, very prestigious and drama free. The family of origin had nothing to do with this it was all on me choosing this mate. Molech had captivated my entire being. I started the cycle all over again, endless relationships with no emotional attachments. I began to struggle with friends and relatives who did not want to watch my child. At one point, I felt these spirits came to rob me of my peace. I questioned my very existence and thought I would not make it. It seemed that everywhere I turned I was in a closed box with no air to breathe. I had been walking in the enemies lies, and with much ignorance, my grave got deeper. There was no one to rescue this lost young woman. The maze intensified and I further yielded into the hands of Satan. The winding slope to his traps thrust me into death row, sentenced to life in prison. Molech had won!

Chapter 4

Paroled: 7-time Felon

Calling docket number 012578, please step forward. Your charges read that you have been convicted, as a 7-time felon, of seven counts of murder, how do you plea? "Guilty," I responded. Guilty for all the years of walking in the dark, and crying countless nights to be delivered and set free. For wondering if I was deserving of being loved, or craving the touch of someone else who could care and see that I was a really good person who made immature decisions. With the lack of guidance and following the path most traveled, I was placed on death row, walking through the valley of the shadow of death. The vapors of sin were so gruesome that I could not find any resemblance of the young woman I once knew anymore. I was convicted of losing my vibrancy and vitality when the evil spirit of murder came into me. The strongman of murder came with poisonous ivy that flowed out to everything I touched. Murder is a big umbrella, and the works of the flesh fall under this umbrella. The strongman needed to be uprooted and dislodged so that the other spirits could be eradicated. The reality is, every morning I would get up and go to work, barely existing as the fierce winds blew the tears on my face. Tears of anguish and resolve, which was my portion and life, was succumbing to the forces operating against me. Who was I fooling, no one but myself. I am guilty of hoping this cycle would end.

The friends that were around were not my real friends. All I heard was a lot of jesting and criticism. These people began to turn their back on me and spread my business to those who were not my allies. They started to talk about how reckless I was and how I would always get what I deserve. I felt like I was in a coffin, not able to feel my arms or face. Molech had set me up to fall again. I was a worshipper of Molech, a god who numbed me to the point that I made abortions a remedy for birth control because of my reckless behavior. My default behaviors always surfaced in a new relationship, but the men were different. It was the same spirit inside of me which caused the same result. Many of us want to be in a happy relationship but how can we expect something good to come if the same spirit governing us still exist and we are the same person. Everything presented was so simple as long as I worshipped and continued in the child sacrifices. I would not have the headache of rearing a child, baby father drama, wedlock or being on public assistance anymore. Once an untainted girl and now a mere vapor in a distant silhouette rolled away on a stretcher into the recovery room. When Saul now Apostle Paul was on the Damascus Road he was faced with a life-altering encounter. I too was met with a life-altering encounter. Appearing at my bedside seem to be a kind face saying, "You do not know me, but I know you. I heard your cry for help, and am here to deliver you out of this dungeon." This dungeon is where I heard the screams and torture of those who never made it out alive. Those who never woke up out of the anesthesia, but found Molech not only took the child sacrifice, but the life of the mother taken as well.

The countless mothers, fathers, boyfriends, husbands, friends, bishops, evangelists, pastors, elders, and the whole fivefold ministerial leaders that accompanied women to get rid of their babies was prevalent. It was the norm to cover and hide, and no one would ever find out. There was a screeching cry of the souls who still feel the guilt and shame of this very thing, murder! While in an out of anesthesia, the touch of this person seemed so real. She was the prettiest person I had seen in a long while. She was so gracious, gentle and kind, with a touch that was so warm and soothing to those who were broken hearted. This person stayed with me until I was fully conscious and awake. "Do Not Come

Back Here," the voice said. At this moment, the dark cloud and the spirit of murder or should I say abortion was broken off of my life. I no longer had to face the trauma of killing babies anymore because someone greater loved me. He knows all of my sins and that I am worth the visitation. Could God send someone in my place of being lost and even at the slaughterhouse? I asked, "Who are you?" The angel responded, "I was sent to fight for you and to give you a message to save my people who are in the same position. Go and tell all those men and women faced with this same crime that their shame and guilt is forgiven. If they ask me to forgive them, the I AM that I AM is faithful to save and deliver." This angel proceeded, "Go tell the youth that there are diseases and sicknesses set as a trap to keep them defeated. Tell my people that the Father has open arms to heal their pain, shame, rejection, their brokenness and to flush them of the residue placed on them." As I left there, I could feel a strong determination that things would get better. I wrestled with the idea of how I would be able to prove the Lord visited me.

How would I be able to tell them that there is information, knowledge, and wisdom readily available for those that needed freedom?

Hosea 4:6

"My people are destroyed for lack of knowledge: because thou hast rejected knowledge, I will also reject thee, that thou shalt be no priest to me: seeing thou hast forgotten the law of thy God, I will also forget thy children."

At that moment, I could hear the sound "tell my people." I uttered in my heart, oh Lord, please do not forget those that are perishing. Lord, even if it hurts I will tell them. Also if I am exposed, I will take up the task. Even though I was not ready to tell the people, I kept on prolonging and did not want to sound the alarm. In a daze, I did not want to step back into the psyche of remembrance. I wanted the memories to be a figment of my imagination; to compartmentalize the years of this part of my life. I wanted it all to disappear, as I started feeling that I could not share what was happening. How could I prepare myself to be put on display for the commentators to assassinate me further? As time progressed, I grew further away from the reality of what took place. Acting as if the encounter never took place, I began to mask and live life. I continued to walk with my head up high and avoid anything that reminded me of the past. However, I began to study further on the effects of abortions and read literature on the graphic procedures. Astonished by the detrimental side effects of abortion and the mental torment. Depression, pseudo happiness, deep voids, and a wedge had many in the state of avoidance. There would be recurring dreams of women screaming and some even drowning in an abyss. I saw in the dreams many strangled by an umbilical cord which represented their past. I could vividly see men standing, trying to cut the cords, but instead grabbed and attached to them. The dreams kept coming, and I knew it was confirmation that for such a time as this, God wanted my voice to permeate the earth, to silence the trauma and the voices of the adversary in and through them.

I began to study the history of abortions. Uncovering the process of the procedure and the legalization of it globally was devastating. In countries such as the United States and China, the numbers were shocking. Abortion was a modern day holocaust. In that time, the Jewish people were slaughtered and persecuted by Adolf Hitler. I will not go into the political tensions surrounding abortions, but I want to bring awareness to the spirit of Molech. The trick of the enemy regarding pregnancies is during 8-12 weeks they call it a blood vessel or tissue. Many pro-choice people feel the suction aspiration method is less invasive. However, the truth is that at 8-10 weeks, developments are happening rapidly of the fetus or embryo. The eyelids have begun forming, hair appears, the child may even suck its thumb, do summersaults, flips, smile amongst more. By week 14 muscles lengthen, week 15 taste buds develop and at week 16 the child can grasp with his or her hands. The fetus can hear and recognize their mother's voice between week 18-20. But these developments are sharply interrupted often by Salt Poisoning (Saline Injection), Prostaglandin Chemical Abortion (chemicals causing severe contractions), Hysterotomy or Caesarean Section (usually performed the last three months of pregnancy). Guided by ultrasound, the abortionist will grab the baby's legs with forceps and pull it out of the birth canal. The abortionist then delivers the baby's entire body, except for the head. Taking a pair of scissors, they will jam it into the babies' skull, which often enlarges the skull. The scissors are removed, replaced by a suction catheter. The baby's brain is then sucked out, causing the head to collapse and killing the baby.

This procedure is very gruesome, but there are times when the fetuses are removed out of the body while still alive. In this case, they are left unattended to die due to neglect or exposure. To think that Molech infused my heart and filled it with Novocain so I could not feel. I chose not to hear the sound of the heartbeat, or see the sonogram. I refused to get attached emotionally to what was alive inside me. The emotional detachment was necessary to move on. There was no time for tears or emotions. Whether pro-choice or pro-abortionist opinions, I felt that the early stage procedures were the best and less life-threatening. No one ever told me that there would be scarring, a buildup of tissues that could cause cervical cancer, thinning of my cervix or complication of having another baby. All abortion options are a near-death experience. You choose at your own risk just like choosing to swim in a pool without a lifeguard. Abortion was, is and continues to be deadly and horrible.

I stand with those who have suffered in silence. Those who did not have someone to talk to. I genuinely feel your pain and share your sentiment. I am saddened by our loss and the ignorance of others who have condemned those who have decided to judge, ridicule, tear down and cast away. There is a Healer who can touch all of our infirmities, meaning he feels and knows what we all go through whether good, bad or indifferent. The Healers touch restores life and heals all wounds if you allow him. You are no longer in prison or in the chains that have hindered your advancement. He came to give life to set the captives free. He is the restorer of the breach. Jesus Christ has made room at the foot of the cross for both you and me. So if you do not feel deserving of the Father's love, that is a lie from the pit of hell. Our Father loves us. He sent his only begotten Son Jesus to save us from all sin, destroy the works of the devil, and to reconcile us to the Father. He sent a comforter, a friend that is closer than any brother or sister. A Paraclete, one who walks alongside us, an advocate, our defense all through God the Holy Spirit. Who is a person, the third person of the Holy Trinity. He convicts and leads us into all truths So my friend if I can ask that you take a moment right now and ask the Father to heal you and deliver you from all guilt, rejection, and shame. He will forgive and place all that we have done in the sea of forgetfulness. The bible clearly states in Roman 8:1-2, "There is therefore now no condemnation to them which are in Christ Jesus, who walk not after the flesh, but after the Spirit; for the law of the Spirit of life in Christ Jesus hath made me free from the law of sin an death."

Forgiveness is hard for some people. The bible talks about us forgiving others continually, but how do we forgive ourselves for all the wrong we have done? If we ask The Father in Heaven to forgive us, then we can forgive ourselves. I stand in the gap for each one of you. Take yourself off the hook and receive liberty. If the Father of truth can do it for me, he can do it for you. My Father and your Father in heaven is not partial.

Salvation is a gift and is readily available, receive the Father by faith. You do not need a mountain of faith to believe; only believe. I feel compelled to pause from writing at this point because HIS anointing to break every chain and destroy every form of bondage is present. Have a one on one with the Father right now and be refreshed to proceed. You see my dear friend I love every one of you. It is not so much the words that will follow on the pages to come, but your soul and reconciliation to the Father which is what matters most to me. If you have any blockages that need removal, I command them to go, so that your life will change from lesser to greater. We cry out to the one who can do all things well, the God of the universe. He knew you would be reading this book right at this moment. He knew that he had to send this writer to stand and intercede for your broken heart and pray you through at this point. You are about to see your life leap bountifully and you will begin to see the light at the end of the tunnel. I am no longer a lost girl but redeemed by the precious price he paid because of His everlasting love. You are His beloved, and He extends the hands that have never failed to lift you to sit at the Kings table. Hallelujah! Isn't our God Awesome? He is mighty to save, mighty to restore, mighty to give you an expected end. May your life and heart be uplifted as you continue to the next part of what My God has and continues to do in my life, BE FREE!!! Read on.

Part 2: Room #2

Processed in the Dark Room

God's processing you in His darkroom,
A place of concealment and obscured light,
A period of progressive development,
As He begins to transform you at midnight!

A place of hidden illumination,
Void of all color except the blackened rays,
You are a negative in His camera,
Who will soon experience bright-less days!

He's protecting you from exposure,
So that you won't have to be destroyed and of no use,
A film of captured purpose and contentment,
One who will overcome satanic abuse!

A time of separation and forming,
Not easily explained or understood,
He'll immerse you in acidic conditions for
transformation,
Not for evil, but for your good!

He'll put you in His secret place,
In the shadows of His wings,
A picture in the making,
While going through spiritual burns and stings!

There's an image in His mind,
That only God Himself can see,
He'll say, "Soak a little longer,
Until you look like Me"!

Processed in the Dark Room
While in the darkroom,
You take a glimpse at the olive-green safety-light,
A color of an embittered-hopeful experience,
A glare blocking your sight!

It is certainly a mystery
Why God has you in there for so long,
I guess He's beautifying your attributes,
And making you spiritually strong!

He draws you out of the wet solution,
As an outline of a new person begins to appear,
Touched by His creation,
His heart releases a joyful tear!
Now that you think you're ready,
You tell God that you want to be shown to everyone,
He then tells you, "Not just yet my child,
There's still work to be done"!
He then clips your photograph,
On a line for your flesh to hang and dry,
A snap-shot in fruition,
That He cannot deny!

He takes you in His hand,
And looks at you with an inspecting scope,
He breathes a sigh of relief,
When He detects an image of hope!

PROCESSED IN THE DARK ROOM
He looks a little closer,
To see you face to face,
You wonder how you made it through this transition,
Nothing but a reflection of His grace!

He says to you, "You're finished now,"
As He frames you and handles you with care,
An unrecognized sight to marvel at,
As the crowd is compelled to stare!

PROCESSED IN THE DARK ROOM
Stephanie B. Ford
02/17/05

Chapter 5
My Vow, 1999

When you make a vow, all parties expect that each person will keep their part of the agreement. There are specific vows that we make with people that are concealed by grace and mercy. Looking back over the past few years of my life, I am finally here. Where? My final year of college at John Jay College for Criminal Justice. I decided to shift my focus to get my life in order. My drive in school allowed me to block out some distractions. During this time, there was no desire to party, entertain friends, dating, having sex, or participate in activities that would waste my time. I reminisced about my visitation in the recovery room, and the heartbreak I went through. The man that I was in a relationship with never took me seriously even after being pregnant by him twice. He avoided me during my process, and I recall telling him, but he never believed me. He probably was happy that I never went through with the pregnancy. At this point in my life, I completely shut down. I noticed friends were no longer friends anymore. They stopped inviting me to places, even though I was known as the 'fun one.' My home was no longer the hangout spot. No one was by to eat, celebrate, or get their hair done. I began to feel a tearing away inside of me, and a tearing apart from people. Every night I would go to sleep and wake up at the same time each night. The digital clock would always read 11:34 pm. Night after night, I woke up at the same time. I found this to be very weird as it went on for several months. Then one night, I flipped the clock upside down and the time was in reverse. The word HELL, minus the semi-colon, was staring back at me. I began to get an eerie feeling. It was as if the clock was talking to me.

I had a friend whose mother kept a church in her house in Brooklyn. I remember because, during my party days, we all would go to the club on a Saturday night, then go to my friend's house and spend the night. The next morning her mom was having church in the living room. This specific Sunday, I knew I had to visit that church, especially after seeing the clock. That day during service, a couple of us were laid out on the floor. The Pastor prayed for us and anointed us with oil in her living room. I did not understand much of what was going on, but I do remember that I had a calling from God on my life. I needed God to erase the past. The wrestling and toiling began to intensify, as I made a vow to God. A vow that I would not give of myself, and be celibate allowing God to purge me. My heart was devastated, and I often found myself crying, experiencing moments of deep sadness and travail. I was lied to, cheated on, talked about, laughed at, wounded, bleeding to death, and left for dead. I thought how a person could be sorry and still do the listed things above. See an opportunist will only do what you allow them to do. Once their mission is accomplished, they discard people from their lives. Then it hit me! I was getting a dose of my own medicine, the same thing I did countless times to men in the past. Their actions forced me to gather my faculties quickly and commissioned myself to become better versus bitter. In that moment of time, the process of healing was taking place. It was the time where I had to get to know Nabiha in a greater way. That no man can love me the way God can. I began to pay close attention to my body chemistry. I no longer had the scents of others or desired to be in an intimate relationship during this process. This was another life-altering moment for me. I needed to get a clear indication that if I did not take heed of this process, I would have missed my breakthrough. I would have been damaged goods and no good to anything or anyone.

It was a time where all that I strived for was finally working in my favor. However, I thought if I dotted every 'I' and crossed every 'T', it would end there. I was sadly mistaken! To my surprise, it was another world opened to me. It was the world of opening up to self-awareness. I should have stayed behind the smokescreen, or perhaps maybe I should have remained on the hamster wheel because this new 'vow' seems to be costing everything in my life to disappear.

December 1999 was the year of life and death, being betrayed, and the year leading up to many years to come of revelation of my life and destiny. As I began to assess my life, I noticed so many variables that contributed to me being a lost black girl. One of the factors, which caused much deficit, was the lack of love from my mother. It was the hardest thing to face because I have a beautiful mother who worked, provided, and kept a roof over our head. She did all that she could to keep us stable, healthy and fed. However, what my mother did not understand is that she never told me how much she loved me. I was not aware that you needed to hear it, feel it or demonstrate it. She showed her love by working a 4 pm -12 am shift, to and from her state job. She would always have a cooked meal on the stove for us to eat when we came home from school. I began to see the cycle of rejection did not just start with my mother. This cycle started generations prior. It started when my grandmother left my mother and siblings in

Guyana to come to the United States. My grandmother came to prepare them for a better life. My mother stayed behind in her grandparents and late father's care.

My mother later shared that she never heard the words 'I love you' and that she never felt the true love of her father. The only love she felt was from her maternal grandparents. Both my grandmother and mother faced similar situations in life, having to provide for their children and forced to work endless hours. They knew how to provide and care for their children whether they said I love you or not. I thought it was normal to have a hard-working parent, who took care of the daily needs. However, not hearing the words 'I love you' can be the greatest harm to a child.

The Maslow Hierarchy of Needs:

Maslow's (1943, 1954) hierarchy of needs is a motivational theory in psychology, a five-tier model of human needs, often depicted as hierarchical levels within a pyramid.

Maslow stated that people are motivated to achieve individual needs and that some needs take precedence over others. Our most basic need is for physical survival, and this will be the first thing that motivates our behavior. Once that level is fulfilled the next level up is what motivates us, and so on https://www.simplypsychology.org/maslow.html.

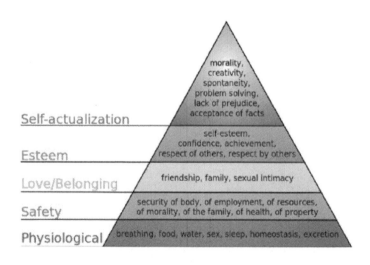

Maslow, A. Motivation and Personality (2nd ed.)
Harper & Row, 1970

This chart is essential because it illustrates what we all need in every stage of our lives and if one component is not present, and then we have missed a vital piece to our emotional composition.

Sometimes in life, the most intense pain comes from those in our own family, those closest to us. In May 2000, I graduated from John Jay College with my Bachelor of Arts degree. It was such an overwhelming experience but yet exciting time. Rolling back the curtain of memories, I began to see family in a different light. There was less engagement with my family, as their support was very minimal as of lately. I started to see an individualistic set of people, who I had to make an appointment to see. It was no longer an organic relationship, and I was estranged from them at this point. Moments of shame kept on coming back to me. I no longer felt as if I could fit in with friends and I learned during the real essence of true friendship. Friends were not the people who come into your home and steal your clothes, instead of asking. I would freely give to a friend if they were in need. The same type of care and love I gave to others, I was not getting in return.

One day, I said a prayer, telling God to remove all unfriendly friends that mean me no good. I disconnected from anything that reminded me of the lost black girl. It was time for sobering. This type of sobriety was not the one that rids the body or alcohol or drugs. It was the type where you reflect and embrace the journey that lies ahead. I never had to drink alcohol before when I was hanging out; I was a free-spirited and carefree person getting high off life and excitement. I can recall an earnest conversation I had. It was during a car ride with a friend about settling down, getting my life together. Little did she know she was depositing a seed of salvation. I could feel sexual lust dying, a purging taking place, and the process and cleansing in my inner being and getting in touch with the girl, I once knew. I had to dig deep and wide to find that jovial, loving and dominant girl I was when I was in school plays, the color guard, and the booster/cheerleading squad. The girl who was so kind and caring of others. I had to embrace all that I had done and begin to seek higher intervention. Looking back on the journey, I knew I had to go back to all the places where I encountered Molech and declare, "I am never coming back to that awful abortion table." I had to visit the multiple locations independently on several trips to confront my fear, the sleepless nights of shame, and to experience freedom from the grave, prepared for me by Molech. I had to face death, confront its ugly face, and say this chapter to murder is now closed.

I would hear of young girls who set their appointments but later walked out to continue with their pregnancies. They mentioned that they were not for sure if the fathers would be there to support, or how things would turn out, but I was encouraged they were liberated and sparred from the gruesome process. I wondered if I deserved another chance. My last procedure deemed me as not being able to bear another child, and if I did, I could miscarry. After that final abortion, I had abnormal cells developing in my cervix, and I underwent a Cryosurgery. This procedure consists of freezing the cells with liquid nitrogen for the removal of unhealthy cells. I remember after having this procedure, and while walking home feeling as if my uterus was falling out. I began to have hot and cold flashes, dizziness, and my body felt weak. I knew the many abortions I had caused my cervix walls to weaken, but the God I serve is faithful and just to forgive, restorer of the breach. I refused to believe that I could not have children again. God is the one who is there when you cannot find anyone. I was not sure if I had all the answers to move forward. You never know what you are made of when faced with a test. Nabiha will you pass the test? I thought to myself I cannot take any more tests, I am flunking already, but there is always more when the teacher is teaching.

Chapter 6

Dead End: Death and Life, 2001

There are certain seasons in our life that we must pay close attention. When and how certain things come into our lives is important. In school, teachers teach students in various subjects, and then assess their readiness for promotion to the next grade. I was a poor test taker, but better at writing essays. I never liked the pressure of someone standing over me. I felt that a teacher could not understand the anxiety a student feels when taking a test. To pass onto a higher level, it is necessary to study, learn and master each subject. If you do not study and pass the test, you then have to repeat the grade or subject level. During a test, the teacher never provides the answers. You have to bring to remembrance all you have learned during your study time. In life, test will come sporadically, in most cases you are not given time to prepare for life's test. Tests can come in various forms, such as strength, mental ability, physical, academic, and spiritual. Spiritual test come to help develop patience, perseverance, and character. To sharpen our proclivities and abilities to be a better

66

person. Each person has unique survival mechanisms within him or her. I believe the Lord has placed many survival strategies within me. I experienced many battle scars and wounds from what I have been through growing up. We as people, have tenacity and resilience to overcome, endure, and pass multiple test in life. There will be times where we have to count our losses and embrace the fact that something may have not worked out the way we planned. However, setbacks and disappointments do not equate to being a failure. There are events in life that come along to test us. They may occur like a cycle. For example, there might be a particular situation, occurring each year around the same time. I know for me, there are specific cycles in my own life and I try to understand why they occur.

In my life, it seemed that every April or May something epic was always taking place. Whether it was something that came to deter or hinder my advancement or a time where I experienced breakthroughs and successes. One Sunday morning, I woke up feeling well and went to work. I recall visiting my son's paternal grandmother and having a discussion with her and my son's father. I remember telling them I did not mind them having a relationship with my son. I wanted to keep the peace and come to terms with what happened in the past. As I spoke to them, there was such an eerie feeling in my stomach. At the time, my son's father was released from prison for attempted assault and violating an order of protection. In my mind, I wanted to give him a chance to build a relationship with his son. I thought that we were both adults and could have a productive conversation. I left my son with him for a little bit, so that they could bond. On my way back to the house, I was on the phone with my sister and I said, "I feel something bad is going to happen. She stayed on the phone with me while he brought my four-year-old son down the stairs. I saw a blank and distant glare in his eyes that I had seen in times past when he was violent or drunk. This look indicated that he had premeditated what he was about to do. All I heard him say was, "B****, I want to talk to you." I responded, "For what?" He placed my son in the back seat of the cab and reached over snatched the cell phone from my hand, and pulled me out the cab by my hair. I resisted and he became extremely physically abusive toward me. He began punching me in my face hard. Blow after blow and thrash and after thrash.

Let me rewind to a couple of weeks prior, I started seeking God and attending church weekly. I visited a few church services and felt uplifted each time. I was in pursuit of getting my life in order and seeking solace in God. I was falling in love with Jesus and trying to live for him. Now going back to that night on April 21, 2001. He knocked me to the ground and he kept punching me in my face. He seemed to focus solely on my face because my body was not hit. I heard the screeching of tires as the cab driver drove off and left me there fighting for my life. I was in so much shock because what human being would do such a thing. All I could hear was my son crying and he too was pushed to the ground. "If I can't have you, no one else can", his father yelled. At one point, his family members came outside screaming, "Stop, Stop, STOP, you are going to go back to jail." That did not seem to deter him; he was like a ravenous animal so enraged with anger. He was full of hate, rage and violence. This all seemed to be unreal to me as he entered into the realm of being a possible murderer. I began to feel my consciousness slip away. In and out, every time he hit me, I saw shots of flashes of light, which looked like lightening. I felt the life in me drift away, my body, and then my spirit became limp. I remember my face hitting the side of the curb and he began to kick me in my head repeatedly. As I laid on the ground, it was as if my spirit left my body and I was looking down at me on the ground.

I could not remember what was happening, but there was an inner cry for Jesus to rescue me. While transitioning in and out of consciousness I could feel my spirit leave my body and began to travel to hell, and then travel to heaven. During that transition, I saw a vision of hell and heard many people screaming and crying. Then my spirit travelled to heaven, and I saw images of different types of angels. It did not look like the heaven that is shown on television. This was a calm waiting place. I felt the tugging on my arms and my heart, as sudden fear came over me. I thought am I really dead as my body was still lying on the ground. I did not know how long my body laid there but it felt like a lifetime, as I waited in this transitioning place. In the midst of this outer body experience, I could see my body lying on the cool curbside as my face was kicked and stomped. I heard Jesus say "Are you ready to serve me now Nabiha?" I replied, "Yes, Lord."

I woke up with the police officers by my bedside who immediately started asking me questions. I later found out that a couple was coming home from a party around 2:00 AM and saw my son pulling me to safety. The father fled and left me there to die. His family who lived right on that block did not come to my rescue. Oh my Lord! How could the baby I did not want just be the vital lifeguard in my time of need? God has a funny way of dealing with each one of us. When I asked for a mirror, there was so much hesitance, but with much persistence, I began to see only black and blue marks.

My face was swollen and unrecognizable. As I laid there in my hospital bed, the tears started coming down. My eyes were now bloodshot and filled with tears I could not even see what was in front of me. I had a fractured nose and my face felt like raw meat. I looked around for my son and I saw him sitting in a chair safely. I was so thankful for his safety, and that Child Protective Services did not receive notification about the incident.

I knew in this moment there had to be a complete surrender to God. I remember working for the Bronx District Attorney's office and sharing an office space with a woman. She was so gracious, she came to see me by my mother's home and she prayed for me. She also presented me with a Women's New International Version Bible. Within two weeks' time, my face was healed and my nose was back in place. There were no signs or traces of any bruising. The only thing that remained, was a little bump I feel on the bridge of my nose as a reminder that Satan did not kill me. God was there in the midst of testing. My life was at a critical point and I needed a mighty touch. God was showing me his healing power. I knew that when my spirit came back in my body I was ready, but I began to feel my pull all over again.

I was now planning a trip to party in South Beach, Florida with friends. I did not fully surrender to God at this point, but I knew my time was coming quickly to yield to the inevitable. I met up with my friends when I landed in South Beach. We immediately hit the strip and walked to all these different places. We were having such a great time until I saw some familiar faces. I'm thinking to myself how the heck is my sons' father's family down in South Beach the same time as me. We all locked eyes and they ran up to me, ready to fight. I was not afraid of them, but I was embarrassed by their behavior. This was outrageous! They blamed me for my son's father being on the run from police. They didn't care what he did to me and my child, they were willing to aide in all his wrongdoings and they made that clear to me. From that day on, I terminated all communication and to his family, never allowing them to see my son.

My son did not have a relationship with them from the age of four until he graduated from high school. They proved they could not make sound decisions about my child and his upbringing. The only way they could have access to my son was when he turned eighteen years old. I knew what God delivered me from, and all of this was God cautioning me that it was time to serve him. My house was robbed while I was away on vacation, and I did not feel safe. My son's father was still on the run from police and I needed to move immediately. There were folks who suggested I move in with them, but I wanted to live on my own and not with others. I did not want people around me, commenting on my every move. I wanted my privacy but was willing to receive good counsel when it came to moving forward in my life. I admit, I was at a place where I needed direction and guidance, because my life was spiraling away.

I was still attending church services, trying to work on living my life right for God, but I seem to fail each time. Even though my last relationship did not turn out well, someone new came into my life. He was very kind, and such a gentleman. We spent a lot of time with each other and it naturally turned into a committed relationship. He was dear to my heart, but I began to see that he did not have the capacity to deal with a woman who had a child with special needs. He was a hardworking man and helpful, but the problems with my son created conflict between the both of us. My son had many meltdowns and it just became too much for this man. "Your son is an animal", he said. I was in shock. I could not comprehend how this man was so kind and nice to me but cold and heartless towards my son. "I love you, but not your son", he yelled. It was like a slap in my face. I know my son required help, but he was still a child.

There was one incident, when my son was erratic and out of control. He needed to be restrained and was placed in an ambulance and taken to the hospital. There were so many issues with him. Multiple schools kicked him out and no one wanted to watch him. I was at wits end trying to figure out how to get this child help. It seemed every place I would go and call was a dead end. On multiple occasions, I would call out from work as a High School teacher, just to take care of him. When he became a problem. Molech would whisper that I should have killed him, and I would have been free from all the misery. Granted, that choice could have been the easiest, but the Lord knows there was a better plan.

My relationship was now hanging on a string, and very strained. I thought that if my lifestyle would change that things would fall into place. I knew something was missing in my life, because I could feel a greater pull towards God. The situation with my son got worst. There was no evaluation, or help that could prevent what started taking place. I did not think that demons were real. My son began to manifest in some extreme behaviors. His speech changed at times, similar to what is portrayed in paranormal movies. My son started to look possessed, and he was not his normal self for a young child. He seemed to be undergirded with the strength of a grown person. What was really happening?

Am I to blame for what is happening to my child? I started to wonder if my actions from the age of 15 opened the portal for these forces to come. Molech wanted my seed that was living. He wanted my son to be a part of that human sacrifice ritual. Family and friends could not help me in this situation. I needed the LORD to help me with this as I was at a dead end.

Chapter 7

Come to a prayer meeting, 'it' will change your life

Since he was a toddler, my son was manifesting strange oppositional behavior. The behavior was one of a child with severe emotional challenges. There was difficulty finding a daycare that would keep him. One daycare, called me fifteen minutes after I dropped him off. "Please come back and get your son. He cannot stay here," she said. At other daycares, there were episodes of my son tearing up the whole house and tormenting the adults that would come around. All of this was becoming too much for me, as no one wanted to deal with my son. He was a liability to their establishment, mainly because other children were around. My sister, grandmother, mother, and a couple of friends were the only ones that would help. It seemed like my son's behavior was disrupting our lives. I moved around a lot, taking safety precautions so that his father would not find us.

Some of my closest friends knew that I was having a hard time with my son. One day, I received a call from my son's godmother. "Nabiha, why don't you bring your son to church for deliverance?" I remember the conversation like it was yesterday. She assured me that Jesus would be there and my son would receive healing. She invited me to her church in downtown Manhattan near Wall Street. I did not think twice, I immediately got myself together and headed to the train station. I took the #4 train from Yankee Stadium in the Bronx to the Fulton Street in Manhattan. When God wants to get your attention, He will use the closest thing to get to you. This thorn in my flesh was constant and unbearable. It was causing much depression and hopelessness. It was a Friday night, and my heart was open to divine intervention. I have had multiple people let me down thinking they knew how to help me with my child. I was tired of the endless money spent on childcare and the amount of time each day spent to get my son stable. "God if you deliver this boy I will serve you," I said. I prayed this repeatedly. God was setting me up for something more significant.

That summer a shift took place in my life. It was time to return to school and teach, but I needed one more state certification and a passing grade in the Content Specialty Test (CST) to keep my job. I took both exams and failed. My next step was to apply for unemployment, but even that became problematic. Someone was receiving my checks and cashing them. All of this was happening while my son was still behaving out of control. One day, I took him to St. Vincent Hospital for an evaluation. They told me that they would have him under observation and release him after. There had to be something more they could do. I suggested that they keep him, as I did not want him to come back home. The treating doctors suggested medication as a solution. I was against medication from the beginning, but they convinced me that it could help him. I consented to him receiving Depakote, Concerta, Zoloft and other psychotropic medications. When it was time for his discharge, we left and went back home.

What was about to happen was something out of a horror movie. At home, I had one of my college friends come over to visit. We were downstairs, and my son was upstairs in his room. We were talking and catching up on old times when all of a sudden there was screaming from upstairs. I ran up the stairs and stood at the top watching my son cry out of control. He was having an adverse reaction to the medication. When he heard me say I was taking him back to the hospital, he ran out of the room towards me and pushed me down the flight of stairs. He leaped from the top of the stairs to the bottom where I was on the ground. He began to bite and gnaw at my right thumb. My nail separated from my skin and blood started squirting all over the walls. My friend watched in shock and became nervous. My son seemed to act as if he wanted to murder me.

There was a spirit of violence and vengeance in his eyes. He seemed to be in a trance and started attacking anything that represented Jesus. There was an eerie feeling that came over me. The impression I felt back when I was on the abortion table and when his father was attacking me. It was as if a dark agent was hovering over my life and would not let go of its grip on me. If I would have put up a resistance and used force against my son at that moment, I do not believe I would be at a place to write this book. I watched as he began tearing up the house. Anything that was in his way he destroyed. It was as if I was watching the Warner Brothers cartoon with the Tasmanian devil. "The blood of Jesus," I screamed. He looked at me with devilish eyes and yelled, "Don't say that F****** name Jesus." I did not stop, I kept saying it repeatedly, and he took his hands and covered his ears. When the police and ambulance finally arrived, my son was sitting at the bottom of the stairs looking angelic as if nothing took place. I escorted him to the ambulance and went to the emergency room for treatment. They gave me a tetanus shot because he bit my skin off. When I later spoke to my friend, she told me that if she was not present, there was no way she would have believed what took place because it was unreal at the time. When my son was in the hospital, I called my family and shared that after this incident, I did not want him anymore. I made up in my mind that I would voluntarily place him with the Administration for Children Services (ACS). I met with a caseworker, and in her opinion, putting my child in foster care was not the best choice. She explained that there was an alternative if I would hold on a little longer. She did not know how much craziness this child was bringing to my life. I left that place depressed, feeling alone with no one to help me.

As I laid in my bed, my arm became heavy from the vaccine I received at the hospital. The room was dark, and it just felt cold and dreary. What do I do now, Lord? I did not know the scriptures that well to stand on the promises of God. However, I did remember a story in Genesis about Abraham and his son. Abraham took Isaac to be sacrificed, and God presented a ram in the thicket. The phone rang, and it was my aunt calling from Maryland. She told me that I could sign my son over temporarily to her and he could live with her for some time. When the day came for him to be discharged and go live with my aunt, I purchased a bible for him. In the

Bible, I wrote a note to him and said I loved him. There was a piece of my heart that was numb and hardened toward him. I felt depleted, and once he left, there was so much pain and hurt because I felt terrible letting someone else raise my son. One thing my aunt did tell me and I remember it until today is "Always make sure to put on the oxygen mask first, then you will be able to help others." Riding the Greyhound bus back and forth to visit him was the norm for me. On my visits to see him, sometimes they were happy times and other times not so fortunate. I felt endless moments of extreme shame and guilt about not being in the position to rear my son.

At the time, I was in a relationship and living with my mate. We were not married, but I was still attending church. I would read my bible and study the word daily. After some time, I no longer felt comfortable in the relationship and decided it was time to honor and value my walk with God. One December night, I was getting dressed to attend a Christmas Ball, and we got into an intense argument. The man who was my friend was upset because I no longer had the desire to be sexually intimate with him. He blamed the church for me not wanting to have sex anymore. There were accusations that I was a part of a cult because I was changing and had a desire to be abstinent. We no longer were doing things we used to because I was learning how to love me more and love God. He then cursed at me and cursed Jesus wanting no part of the relationship. We eventually broke up, and I sought God even more. The truth was I had just accepted Jesus into my heart and wanted to start my life all over. I wanted to be set free from all of the pain and chains that bound me. The more I prayed and sought God the more afflictions came my way. I was like a walking infirmary with multiple wounds, bandages, and bruises. Molech did a number on me. I thought that this spirit of shame and humiliation was over. Within four months, everything that was meaningful in my life was lost. I felt as if I missed and failed by not being with my son, losing my job, failing my state boards, having to live in a different unfamiliar place and now the relationship I had learned to be friends first, faithful and stable came to an end.

Now I am single and serving God. I shut myself away from the world and found myself running to church every time it was open. I even cut off friends and family and was on the altar seeking the Holy Spirit. I decided to be baptized, and I soaked up every message preached whether it was from my late pastor or a guest speaker. I no longer sat in the back of the church but moved up to the front so that there would be no distractions. I wanted to be closer to the sound of prayer that came from the altar. What was that sound? It sounded like the voice communing with God. It was the very first time I saw angels. I read about angels but I thought my eyes were playing tricks on me. One day, I heard a sound in the church. It was a sound in prayer. The prayers were coming from the altar. I never heard such a rhythm in prayer. It was as if this person was having a direct connection with the Creator. As I observed the altar, there was only one person on the altar. When I looked, it was my late pastor, praying with the lights turned down low. He often spoke on the importance of reverencing God in the sanctuary. He would tell the people not to grieve the Holy Spirit. He was a man of prayer, and he knew the power of Jesus' Blood and the importance of healing and deliverance. A prayer warrior, who flowed heavily into different realms of the Spirit of God. A general in the Lord's army with much intelligence and knowledge of the word of God. He was a man that provided for his family and never put financial pressure on the congregants. He did not say much and he did not allow you to get comfortable in his presence. Attending that church, I learned so much. The pastor instructed us how to know God for ourselves. He preached that sin could not have dominion in that ministry and attendees reverenced him as a man of God. He taught so many including myself how to walk upright before God, but there was a stern and no nonsense side to him. Anything he felt came to disrupt the church he would address and demand order in the house of God. A father to many, he had the spiritual eyes to see beyond his years. There is so much to say about this oracle of God. The Lord used him significantly as a foundational pillar in my spiritual development and walk with God.

There were so many times I got to church and spent time on the altar before service. It became habitual for me to spend time in prayer. Whether it was at church or home, I was hungry for the Lord. I started feeling the joy and peace of the Lord. I now understand the purpose behind that initial prayer meeting I attended with my son. The Lord used that invitation from my son's godmother to spark the fire within me. Everything that took place in the past was a part of me developing my relationship with God. I grew in wisdom, stature, and zeal for the things of God. I even picked up a strong sense of legalism and began to view everything as demonic. Although I learned a lot from this time in my life, I had to undergo substantial detoxification from the spirit of religion. I developed one having a critical spirit and became judgmental. I no longer wanted to hang around anyone from the world even friends that were genuine to me. In a sense, I was far removed from anything in my past that I did not want to associate with anything or anyone who knew my sins. I had adopted "church friends," and then the cliques started.

I was so out of touch with reality as to why Jesus came and the need for others to be saved. I began to look down on others especially if they were not saved. I did not listen to "secular music," and my speech was always over spiritual. When I prayed, it was from a place of arrogance. I was no longer the lost 15-year-old girl. I was now becoming an adult and believed that everything I did before that time was in the sea of forgetfulness. I no longer identified with things from my past because I walked with a proud look and humility was not my portion. When I began to embrace the prophetic gift on my life, I took things to the extreme. I felt validation because most of the ministers that visited my church would single me out. They all seem to say the same thing, how great the anointing on my life is and how God would use me mightily for his work. It all sounded so good, but I lacked the full understanding of what walking with God at such a level entailed. Would read so many booked on the prophetic gift, as I did not know much about the five-fold ministry of the Apostles, Prophets, Evangelists, Pastors, and Teachers. It is one thing to read about things, and it is another thing to have the experience. All the word I was reading was for vainglory. I started to feel a sense of entitlement every time I read the word of God. I believed that God was entitled to honor his Word in my life because I was serving him.

An incident occurred while my son was in the care of my aunt. While attending a afterschool church program, my son made a sexual advance on another child in the bathroom. My aunt called me frantic asking me where he learned these things. I was clueless and so much was happening while he was living with her. My aunt tried to find the appropriate mental health services and clinical treatment for my son. I remember while in prayer, visualizing a young boy with a heavy backpack and he was heading my direction. The load seemed very staggering and placed him in a posture of straining. As time passed, the monotonous care my aunt had provided for my son began to seem burdensome. It was tough for her to raise another boy in addition to her three other sons. We talked, and the decision was made that my son would be returning to me. The school year was ending, and I was entering into a new place with God. There was a pursuit to find the appropriate educational setting and services for my son. I signed up for parenting skills training and anger management just so that I would be equipped for his return. I created token systems, charts, and decided to have a home of discipline and structure. I did not want an environment where there would be time for idle behaviors triggering his volatile behavior. I was grateful for the day he returned to my care, and I was more thankful that to be given the opportunity by my aunt. She took my son in at a critical time, and I am grateful for the time and effort she put into my son.

As I sit and write, I recall a moment I when I told her I was pregnant. "Will you go and have an abortion," she said. I thought to myself, God you have a sense of humor. The same aunt who initiated the idea of an abortion is the same person to rear him for a period. Molech lost this seed to his fire. We have to be careful of the curses that may pass down from another generation. If I had listened to others and abort my son, I would have missed the vital part he played in me knowing Jesus. I have so many vivid memories while driving up and down on 95 South. There were many tears shed while traveling to seeing my son in Maryland. I was a pain-filled parent, ashamed and embarrassed because I did not love the unwanted child. The depth of this pain was real. I felt the very nature of failing as a parent and failing as a single parent. I was a college graduate with a son who had significant challenges. I needed a job and ended up finding employment within the social service field. There was nothing glamorous about this field at all. It was a field that dealt with marginalized and depraved families. Through the course of working in this field, I realized that I got the understanding of how different systems operate. I was desperate to find out what resources were readily available. I did a lot of research in vast areas. I became a student of the educational, criminal justice legal system, mental health and hygiene entities, and how to write letters and read new material in pursuit of understanding what is out there to families. I had to enter a world using new terminology to be versed in a new area.

Moreover, I was developing a new language of prayer with God concerning my son's return. Before his arrival, I understood there are certain things in the underworld and different things that are present. I needed to seek God on these things. My spiritual eyes were opening, and I could remember at the age of six seeing spirits roaming and trying to embody people. At that time, thinking they were a figment of my imagination, but as the covering cast was lifted off my eyes, I began to listen, smell and see things. I saw movements and heard things as I counteracted them in the spirit realm. The time away from my son granted me the opportune time to listen the voice of God clearly and to experience a greater depth of God on a one on one level. The more I sought God, the more revelation of these forces became clearer. I was able to trace all the way back to when I was younger, and what I thought was imagination was evil spirits desiring to disrupt a person's life. Growing up, my family did not understand the demonic, so it was hard to talk to anyone about this revelation. I had to find many answers laying prostrate before God and soaking in his presence to gain understanding and direction on how to counteract these agents. I studied the scriptures on how Jesus walked in authority and that tormenting spirits came to frustrate and dismantle a person, a region, or jurisdiction. Once confronted, they had no choice but to leave. I saw images of the demons, their shapes, and sizes through my spiritual eyes. They had a smell, and I could smell when they stepped into a room. I began to hear them make noises as they swooshed past individuals. I was in obscurity with the Lord. I developed a lifestyle of fasting and prayer. I grew a momentum in prayer and had intentional intimate time with God. My rhythm with God was succinct, and nothing could penetrate my walk with Him. God and I walked closer and developed a bond that was unbreakable. My time was his time and everywhere I went I was in training. God was training me for what was about to come with my son's return. I will never forget when the Lord showed me my hands, and he began to tell me that my hands are a weapon in the spirit. Looking at my small hands, I underestimated the power. Once I started to use my hands in the spirit, I realized they had significance and power.

The anointing of God makes the difference. When my son returned, the first thing I did was anoint him with oil. That was the entry point back into my home. He seemed to be a different child, the adjustment to school and home was going smoothly. We were on a routine and a set schedule, but it was only, 'the calm before the storm.' One morning, he refused to take his medication and started throwing himself on the floor. He was acting up, and I needed to take him to catch his school bus. We ended up catching the bus, and later on that day, I received a call that there was a case opened up against me at Administrative Children Services (ACS). The school staff would not disclose any information, so I had to wait to hear from Child Protective Services (CPS) to arrive. In my distress, a world of concerns came to me because I was familiar with these situations in my field of work. I have seen cases against parents charged with abuse and neglect. A woman from CPS came to my house. "Your son said that you beat him for not taking his medication," she said. My jaw dropped in complete shock. Immediately the investigator went through my home searching for things to deem me as an unfit parent. They opened an investigation against me for possible child abuse. This had to be a dream or yet a nightmare.

Why was this happening to me? She asked for specific documents which readily available and organized in my file cabinet. I began to build up walls of resentment and feelings of rejection toward my son. He was a problem that would not go away. I felt the pull of disaster and disruption lurking. When the woman left, so many thoughts came to mind about this child. How can I get this child away from me? I did not want him to disrupt my walk with God. My relationship with God was the one thing giving me strength and true meaning.

I was no longer in my routine. Things changed because of this child abuse investigation against me. In addition to the daily responsibilities of caring for my son, I had to attend family therapy and dyadic therapy with him while still active in the church. I sought out spiritual advice from leadership at my church. During a counseling session, they said my son's name meant something demonic and suggested I change it. I thought because it was in the bible that it was a 'biblical' name and that it was ok. "Names have significance," one pastor said. I thought to myself maybe we were not reading the same scriptures that 'Demetrius' was a coppersmith. I did some research on the original language of the Greek. I realized his name meant the 'god of the underworld.' At this point, all I wanted was for my son to be free. It was an uphill battle, one thing after another. Evil spirits were spirits governing his emotions and mind and when he was like that it was as if a different person was taking over this little boy's body. As he continued to take his medication, he was still under evaluation, and further testing was taking place. The clinical team assigned to evaluate him were confused as to why this child is not responding to treatment. One early morning while lying in my bed, I saw a shadow past my bedroom door. I did not immediately jump up out of bed, but I knew something was not right. The shadow was my son; he was entering my room with a knife in his hand. As he walked towards my bed, something appeared to be blocking him from getting close to me. All I could do at that moment was pray inwardly; it was as if words were not coming out of my mouth. "The blood of Jesus," I said in my heart. He began to back up that point. He looked like a murderer standing there. How would I explain this to anyone? Who would believe that a seven-year-old child could do this? He left my room and went to the kitchen. I went after him and asked him if he was okay. There was a switch in his demeanor, and he was back to his usual self. I was not afraid of my son, but the incident showed me the importance of learning the art of warfare in prayer. I learned to pray against certain spirits. The more I saw the manifestation of demonic spirits in the natural, the more I began to bind and loose things against those forces.

Ephesians 6:10-18 came alive, and the word of God began to speak to me about how to counteract the forces of darkness in my life. I had to put on the whole armor of God and keep it on.

"Finally, my brethren, be strong in the Lord, and in the power of his might. [11] Put on the whole armour of God, that ye may be able to stand against the wiles of the devil. [12] For we wrestle not against flesh and blood, but against principalities, against powers, against the rulers of the darkness of this world, against spiritual wickedness in high places. [13] Wherefore take unto you the whole armour of God, that ye may be able to withstand in the evil day, and having done all, to stand. [14] Stand therefore, having your loins girt about with truth, and having on the breastplate of righteousness; [15] And your feet shod with the preparation of the gospel of peace; [16] Above all, taking the shield of faith, wherewith ye shall be able to quench all the fiery darts of the wicked.

[17] And take the helmet of salvation, and the sword of the Spirit, which is the word of God: [18] Praying always with all prayer and supplication in the Spirit, and watching thereunto with all perseverance and supplication for all saints."

In all of the times of adversity, distress, and confusion, God's word was the solution to all my problems. Mother's Day in 2005 was a pivotal moment in my life. My son and I attended church service, and he had an altercation with a teenager. When my son would hear the word 'no' or believed that someone was rejecting him, his behavior became erratic. When I went to see what the altercation was about, my son pulled a pen or sharp object out and attempted to stab me inside of the church. Everyone looked on in disbelief, and the scene inside of the church was out of control. The police and ambulance showed up, and I remember telling them to take my son. I felt strong up until that point when he tried to stab me at church. I was tired of pretending that I had him under control. Being around him was not safe, and I did not want anyone to get hurt while around him. The ambulance took my son to Bellevue Hospital, which is a psychiatric hospital. I told the triage that I had no intentions of taking him back home with me. There was no doubt in my mind he was staying in the hospital until they could find him a suitable place to live. I made some calls to make sure that he was getting the right care. On a call with the Department of Education, I requested a higher level of care from a day treatment program to a residential treatment center. All the thoughts of aborting this child came back to me. The trials and tribulations I went through because of this child had me feeling that I should have gone through with it. I began to believe the words and started to develop great resistance and felt shame and anger toward my son and I was embarrassed to go back to that church. All I could think about was the church people witnessing my breakdown and having much to say about it. I thought a spirit possessed my child and I was stuck with him. At a meeting with the Board of Education, the chairwoman said, "You are the only person who knows what you feel. Own your truth." I began to speak at the meeting, and so many emotions came to the surface. I believe the committee saw my frustration, fear, sadness, pain, depression, and turmoil. They decided to approve my son's admittance into the residential program.

Shame was a normal feeling at this point in my life. My son was now leaving me for a second time, but this time he wasn't going to live with a family member, he was going to live in an institution. This institution he would now call home for many years to come. Deep down my son was a loving and caring person. The shame of seeing him forced to take psychiatric medication and tormented by spirits was a lot to bear as a parent. My shame held me captive at times, and I did not want to see him while he was in the institution. All I wanted to do was love my child and make the right choices in caring for him. I blamed myself for things not turning out as I expected. In my mind, I thought God was ashamed of my decision to send him away. There was always a constant reminder of the shame of my poor choices. Through the years I became tougher, harder, and guarded, hiding from people, so they would not see my frailties. My son entered their special education services, and they were now suggesting he take more medication. Taking more medication did not make sense to me, I fought against their suggested medications. The institution said if I continued to fight them on this decision they would open a case against me for medical neglect. The treatment team was not too fond of me and felt I was combative. They even mentioned I needed therapy and instructed me on parenting. My relationship with the staff at the institution was not pleasant. My demeanor became rigid and rude when I dealt with the team. I did not want the constant reminder of feeling disappointed about my failure to rear my son in my home. No longer was I going into his room, or even allowing him to visit me on weekends. Shutting this part of my life off was my focus. However, the more I felt I was done caring for him, the more strength I received from God. I continued attending church and was active in the ministry. That was the only area of my life that gave me comfort and kept me balanced. A friend asked me to visit another church. This invitation was a ticket to understanding that God indeed called me. It was a Thursday, and the church was having all night prayer. The pastor called me out and ignited the gift of prophecy was ignited within me. Since that day, I was able to flow greater depths of accuracy. There was an impartation, and it was something that I never experienced before. Something new was happening, and I wanted more of it. Even though I attended my home church, I still visited other churches from time to time. Months would pass, and I remember visiting a church and was told, "It is time to shift from your church. If you do not shift now, there will be a scandal." I'm thinking to myself, what scandal? I figured I'm not living an ungodly lifestyle, so I did not fully comprehend what was said. I did not understand at the time the importance of obeying a prophetic warning. That if you did not obey, there would be consequences for not doing so.

In 2005, my church planned a trip to Israel. A group of us traveled to the Holy Land, and from the moment we reached Jerusalem, I could feel the prophetic strongly on me. There was such a presence of God in Jerusalem, and you could feel it in the atmosphere. My pastor saw me, and there was a look of scorn on his face. I did not understand why he would look at me the way he did, because I loved him dearly. I often thought he was always so hard on me and did not want to acknowledge the prophetic calling on my life. Perhaps he saw further or maybe not! The more I grew in God, the greater his presence and anointing could be seen in my life. During this time, I started to desire a Christian relationship. There was a guy who I began dating. The relationship entailed fasting and praying together, and attending places in public. There was much caution, as I needed to check my spiritual gauge and remember that there are danger zones when dating as a Christian. It is one thing to suppress the sexual urges and another to be entirely in control of that area. After some time, the sexual desires began to come back. The day it happened I felt awful and much condemnation. In my church, there were only certain things that you could discuss. There were no discussions about sexual sin, because of their closed-mindedness. In situations like this, the only thing offered was prayer and the doggedness of not bringing leaven or sin into the church.

In 2006, my church planned another trip to Israel and it was a group of 120. This trip included so much more than the one last year. Not only did we visit, Jerusalem, Gethsemane, Temple Mount, Mount Carmel, Via Dolorosa (Stations of the Cross), and Mt. Sinai. We also visited the pyramids in Egypt, Petra in Jordan, and spent the night in the desert with the Bedouin people. There was so much happening on this one trip that it was a lot to take in. We also did a baptismal service in the Jordan River, bathed in the Dead Sea, rode camels and climbed Mt. Sinai, crossed the Red Sea and ate St. Peter's fish by the Sea of Galilee. The entire Holy Land tour experience allowed me to see the Bible come alive. Being in Israel was great for me, but I was carrying around this secret. I already asked the Lord for forgiveness, but it felt as if a dark cloud continued to hover over me. There was a true repentance in my heart, and I turned away from the sin. However, I still felt dirty and unclean. While on this trip there was a very handsome gentleman. A group of us bonded on the trip and began to hang out. He was a part of the group and instantly there was speculation that I was with this married man on a 'church' trip. This new friendship was strictly platonic, and I found it strange that the very appearance of us together in a group gave people the wrong impression. I did not entertain the chatter concerning that situation, as I had what I did back home on my mind. I needed to speak to someone about this, so I decided to share my discretions with an evangelist. She frequented my church at times, and we developed a good relationship. She appeared to be sober and mature in the Lord, so I figured why not speak to her. We talked at length about my sexual experiences. She asked, "Are you dating a married man?" I found that question strange, because I just shared with her everything that was happening in my relationship. I responded, "No, I am not dating a married man." She concluded the conversation by praying for me and giving me some scriptures to read. She counseled me on boundaries within a relationship and share scriptures to help me stay purified and clean. Once we returned from Israel, we were all at JFK airport waiting for our rides to pick us up. My ride to go home came, and as I stepped into the car, I looked back and saw the evangelist. There was a look of disgust on her face as she watched me. This was not the same look she had on her face when she was counseling me in Israel.

A few weeks later, the prophetic warning I received about leaving the ministry, came back to my remembrance. It was a whole year since I received that word. I had a feeling something major was about to happen. On July 19, 2006, the phone rang, and it was my pastor. "Sis Nabiha, I need to see you in my office after bible study," he said. The tone in which he said it, indicated that this was urgent and serious. I never spoke with my pastor in his office before, so I did not know what to expect. I was at Bible study, and all I could think about was this meeting. Once it was over, I went into his office and saw the pastor's wife, assistant pastor and my pastor already sitting down waiting for me. "Do you feel this is the time for you to leave the ministry?", the pastor said. Why was he asking me this? He proceeded, "I can't be pouring out my heart, praying for you and you are here sleeping around with married men in the church and in Israel." Did I hearing correctly? He just accused me of sleeping with a married man in the church and Israel. Before I could even answer or defend myself, a voice came from the phone on his desk. There seemed to be someone on speaker listening to the conversation. The voice was familiar, and it turned out to be the evangelist I spoke with in Israel. In shock, she was accusing me with my pastor. Her accusations against me were far from the truth. It was the most horrific feeling one could endure. There was a lot of back and forth, and the next thing I knew I was being ejected from my church. He said, "You and your son are heading for destruction, and if not careful were both going to die." I retrieved a pre-written resignation letter from my bag and placed it on the desk. "I reject every negative word you are speaking against me," I said as I left the office. My world had come crashing down. The trauma, heartbreak, and devastation were crippling me. It did not stop there, the Sunday after, there was a church members meeting. This meeting was to notify all members that Sis. Nabiha is no longer welcome in the church because she is sleeping with a married man and no one is to be in communication with her from this point on. I was excommunicated and left for dead spiritually. I entered into a time warp and a bubble no one could penetrate. I felt the sting of betrayal. BETRAYAL IS REAL!! And it is PAINFUL!!! I changed my number and did not have any friends. I avoided everyone. The people who told me they loved me, were now crucifying me over and over with false accusations. The relationship I was in came to an end. My boyfriend decided to break up with me after hearing what happened, as he too attended the same church. I was left to suffer the repercussions of a broken heart. There was much depression, rejection, and shame. I lost my vibrancy and was just existing at this point.

A couple of months later, my ex-boyfriend came back into my life and said, "Let's get married. I do not want you to be left down and alone." Our relationship was only for about a year, and there wasn't much friendship between us. I did not want to be alone anymore, so I told him yes. We didn't have a real wedding. It was just us, a pastor, pastor's wife, and a business partner of ours as a witness. No one knew I got married because I did not share this with any family of friends. I was far removed from everyone, and this was my secret to keep. It turned out to be the saddest time of my life. There was a call from my spiritual mother a couple of days later. She told me about a dream she had of a beautiful lady ringing the doorbell and bringing me a basket full of pretty fish.

When she handed over the basket to me, one of the fish popped out its beautiful head. "I reject that pregnancy dream," I said. A couple of weeks later, I found out I was pregnant. I had been so scarred from my experience with my son, that to bring another child into this world was absurd. There were too many things happening in my life, and I thought about having an abortion because I was already dealing with the pangs of rearing my son. In December 2006, I had to go to the emergency room because I was hemorrhaging. The attending physician did an internal and external ultrasound. The results were that I was not pregnant and I felt so much relief. When I got home, I fell asleep, and there was a hand touching my stomach. When I jumped up out of my sleep, I did not see anyone. The phone started to ring, and it was the OB/GYN doctor. They needed me to come into the office. I let them know the results of the ultrasound and that I was scheduled for a D&C. The doctor wanted to draw some blood, and they saw that the numbers were still too high for me not to be pregnant. They did further testing and performed another ultrasound to check if there was a baby. To my shock, they were able to find the baby. There had to be a reason this child came forth at this time of my life. Three months pregnant and going through the motions. I found a new church to attend and sat in the back. Work, home and church were the only three places you could find me. It was my routine and I stuck to it. I was a sad pregnant woman. When I went to church, I would not greet anyone. When I went to work, it was a little different. My coworkers were so friendly and kind. They cared for me and showed it every day they saw me. At first, I was a bit apprehensive because of the wounds I received from people I thought were my friends. However, my coworkers were persistent in showing me love and making sure I was doing well. They didn't know at the time, but their actions were giving me strength. They created an environment at work, that felt like a church home to me. They were not devout churchgoers, but they all had a heart of gold and love. My colleagues were like family to me, the ones who God used to heal my broken heart and nurse me back to my usual self. They gave me a baby shower and loved on me so much during these difficult times.

There was a valuable lesson I learned during this time. Having pride and feeling more privileged than others can cause damage if not corrected. When I was going to my old church, my view of unsaved people was closed-minded. Now, my perspective has changed, and there are no more prejudices. Before, legalism had put me in a religious box, and now I was out of that box. Jesus came to destroy the works of the devil, and if I am joint heirs with Christ, I should be doing the same. During my time of seclusion as a prophetess, I developed a specific discipline and spent time with God. My one on one relationship with God was and is non-negotiable. There were constant talks and intimate time with Him. There were periods of silence, but those moments were a time of fundamental teaching about my journey and spiritual formation. God is more than able to do anything he chooses to do. The hand of God was evident time after time in my life. I understood the true meaning of faith and God gave me a radical faith during this process. The faith to defy every negative thing or impossibility that set limits for me. God began to restructure the way I thought and had me in a place where I had to depend on Him only. There were many questions because a part of me felt he was upset with me. I was still learning about God's grace and His mercy. I once believed that looking spiritual on the outside mattered the most, but that was far from the truth. It is about the matter of the heart. Could God still get glory out of my life? Am I still called to preach the gospel? Does the Lord still love me? These were some of the questions weighing me down. Through it all, God was teaching me and preparing me at the same time. He afforded this time of quietness to prepare me for what was about to come.

From 2006 to 2012, things were shifting in my life. I considered those years to be monumental as much accomplishments were taking place. I was a different person now, and my relationship with God grew deeper. My teaching came from the Rabbi himself, Jesus. The Holy Spirit began to reveal things, and I developed spiritual muscles each day. During this time, I learned much about ministry. The different viewpoints and liturgical practices of the church. These are years that I will never forget, as much training and development took place. God was accelerating the time that was lost, and I was able to confront the past rejection and ejection from ministry. There was true forgiveness in my heart. You will know if you are truly freed from your indiscretions when you are faced with a challenge that forces you to apply all that you have learned. Graduating from seminary school was such a great feeling. Then I went on to study at New York University for Hotel Operations and then began pursuing my doctorate. I was moving along in life, accomplishing so much, but I still had questions. Wondering if the shame was gone entirely or was there some residue remaining. Did I deal with the damage of shame in my life? Was I ready to confront Molech once and for all? I knew that anything hidden would manifest and reveal itself. Shame and Rejection were still there! Sometimes you need to travel a further distance from your normal surroundings to see that there is more to be undone. Go deeper, stretch further and then you will be able to utter liberation.

Chapter 8

The Shame is Over!

Tell your story! I remember early one morning, preparing, praying and getting ready to write out a sermon. For some reason, the original sermon was not ministering to me at first, even though it was in alignment with the Holy Spirit. As I sought God deeper and on the most pressing need for the place and people of God, instantly I got quiet and began to hear the audible voice of God. The spirit of the Lord said to listen! I thought listen to what? As I listened, I began to pay close attention to my heart. Instantly I was led to Proverbs 4:23 *"Keep thy heart with all diligence; for out of it are the issues of life," (KJV})*. The more I listened to my heart; a clear vision came to me of an abnormal heart and a normal functioning heart. I studied the organs and how the brain and heart work simultaneously, with the brain releasing messages to the heart. I thought that maybe what I was seeing was incorrect, but as I listened to my heartbeats, they were rhythmic and then very faint. Continuing in prayer, I began to go over all the events in my past that caused my heart to feel heavy. The trauma and pain were hidden in my heart and there were images of residue. It was dormant and the message for the day was switched.

All this time, I was preaching at different churches and events, but never confronting the issues in my heart. The more I kept my story hidden, the more my heart became hardened. My heart was like stone from the deposits of pain, rejection, hurt, unresolved issues, and great disappointment in my life. The Lord was leading me to discuss the issues of my life in public for the first time. On an assignment at a church in Gastonia, North Carolina, I felt that this could be the opportune time to share my story. What happened in Israel and my ejection from church made me feel so vulnerable. I had compartmentalized so many traumas, that I was just functioning from an abnormal place. My compassion had been lost, and I was really in a fragile state. To share my story, meant I was now opening up about the betrayal. While at the church, I was trying to decipher all that was done to me in my past. My moments of great pain, was being dissolved as I began to share my story before the people. Two of my spiritual mothers were in attendance, and I could feel freedom and deliverance come to me and others as I made my life transparent to those in attendance. The church was sectioned into three particular age groups. God allowed me to minister to each generational group, 1-30, 31-60 and 61-120. Some who had abnormalities in their own hearts.

My experience of being heartbroken was imperative to others being able to break free of the shame and deficits they endured.

They were mishandled and misunderstood. The feelings they experienced in failed relationships, betrayal from close family and friends, sexual abuse, and physical and emotional scars. Each person had a heart that was tender. While speaking, I shared the details of everything, even what the evangelist had done to me as I told what that evangelist had done to me. I often wondered if she really understood the magnitude of the pain, shame and damage she caused in my life. Everything I been through was a blessing in disguise, even though I could not see it. Often times, I hear people call their painful church experience 'church hurt', but the fact and truth is 'hurt is hurt'. We can be hurt in our homes, school, hospital, relationship and so much more. Hurt feels painful, and many people deal and undergo vast changes with the ramifications of being hurt. The way we recover from the hurt, if we ever do is important. Some people deal with hurt by using alcohol, illicit drugs, promiscuous relations, partying, being an over achiever, always on a defense, performance driven, guarded, or even revenge. Running away from the hurt doesn't help the situation either. Changing your location, telephone number and avoiding people only prolongs the hurt, giving it more life. Pain is real my dear friends.

Once the service was over, I felt as if something more was to occur but could not quite put my finger on it. The next day was international day at the conference and there was an apostle from the Bahamas in attendance. As she ministered, I listened to her speak while sitting with my spiritual mother, and friend. The message was about being left for dead and being wounded, instantly I felt myself begin to weep. I did not know why I was crying, but the presence of God was so strong. My spiritual mother tapped me on the shoulder and leaned over to whisper in my ears. "Nabs the evangelist is here," she said. Instantly, I dropped to the floor in the sanctuary, crying out to God. The day before I was ministering on emotional healing, and now today something greater was happening. As I lay on the floor, I could feel inner healing taking place. Rolling back the curtains to 2006, I felt freedom. Over the years, the spirit of the Lord, processed the pride, and arrogance within me. The pain that was built up was now dissolved and I wondered if I was in a place to actually see her face to face. I remember rehearsing in my head, what my first words would be when I saw her again. I wanted to fight her, hurt her so she could feel the pain she put me through, but I knew being spiteful and revengeful was not the answer. I had the fear of God and I knew His word. Vengeance was His and he knows how to handle all matters with those that hurt us. I never wanted to render evil for evil, so I took the bullet that was lodged in my heart for years. I felt the bullet ricochet in so many places, and the fragments were coming out as I laid on the floor. I looked at my shame and rejection in the eye, saying "Molech my shame is over! Molech you have no dominion over me. Your sting and grip is over and off of my life." As I was lying there both of my spiritual parents came over to me and whispered in my ear, "is all un-forgiveness gone and if not let it go." I got off of the floor and went over to the evangelist and said three things in her ear. I forgive you, I release you, and what the devil meant for evil, God turned it around for my good so much will be saved. I went to give her a hug and she said, "Tell me your name again?" When I told her my name and where she knew me from her eyes got bigger. She did not recognize the fractured young woman she counseled in Israel and lied on. She was now seeing a woman of god, a guest speaker at the church she was visiting. This was a feeling of God's redemption and a healing moment. As I walked away, I could hear her crying, and saying "I am so sorry, I am so sorry." The cry was a screeching cry like that of a crow. At that point, all was forgiven and, I had the opportunity to testify the day prior and now I felt I possessed the character of Christ because, of how I handled myself when I saw her.

When God heals, he does all things well and totally. It was a moment, that if I did not undergo healing and deliverance of my pride, hurt and arrogance it would not have been a moment to display God's true forgiveness and healing power. Our reward is always in God, when we trust that he is able to work things out according to his time and perfect will. This particular year, was a year to deal with Nabiha as a leader, one called to the office of a prophet, and a doctor of the Lords church to undergo much rigorous training and development as a global leader. During my classroom time in school at the Nyack College Alliance Theological Seminary, we were asked to do a battery of tests on leadership, personality, and character development. We all were required to participate in counseling during our first semester, and to deal with the leader as an individual. This process would highlight so many blind spots in my life. It was in a cohort designed for each person to really get to know themselves in a better way. It was a very emotional time, as if I was stepping into an operating room prepping for surgery. It was a time of shining the light on all and leaving nothing hidden. This was necessary for each of us in order to be an effective leader. It was a time of our individual and corporate spiritual formation to be developed. The assignments were really not from a practical perspective but experiential. Experiential learning was and is the model used for this doctoral program. When you learn experientially, it is more purposeful, has meaning and depth. So often we read a textbook, and there is no relevance. This course dealt with behavioral intelligence, survey links sent to our colleagues, bosses, ministerial leaders and those in our family for them to assess our leadership capabilities. It is easy to pretend to others who don't know us, but those who are in our lives really can tell the truth, keeping us credible and authentic.

This particular survey is to disclose all the hidden sides that are not on the surface, and is designed to place emphasis on areas that need to be developed and purged. Each person who evaluated us, had to be as honest as possible so it would not be a disservice. This tool was very effective, to see if you can handle the pressure in embarking the task of being a leader who is integral, one who has character, and can handle their home life as well as those in the public. Leadership can be taught! Moreover, we had a licensed marriage and family counselor do a session with us, as well as multiple sessions on soul care, and there was one other thing that stood out the most and it was called a genogram. A **genogram** (pronounced: jen-uh-gram) is a graphic representation of a family tree that displays detailed data on relationships among individuals. It goes beyond a traditional family tree by allowing the user to analyze hereditary patterns and psychological factors that punctuate relationships. This particular data had to be used, as we went to different family members. We needed to confront and interview them on things that have occurred in their lives. It was designed to see if it is still operating in my current behavioral patterns. There is so much to learn when we go back in our family history and become aware of what took place in the generations before us and compare to our current practices.

There was much to confront with my family, and those areas required me to travel multiple times for counseling. Sitting in my doctoral class, and wondering if something was wrong with me, is what led me to counseling. I felt that I had a relationship with the Lord. I fasted, prayed and was living an upright life while helping those in need. However, there was a lack in my heart and life. I wondered during this intense class time, what am I missing? I remember the marriage and family

115

therapist saying, "Shame can be transferred from one person to another." I did not want anyone else's shame, as I was already dealing with my own that felt like it was going on for a lifetime. When the class was over, my professor said "Nabiha, your problem is not spiritual; your problem is emotional deprivation." Did he really just say this to me in front of the entire class? He continued, "I have a woman you need to meet with." I decided to take him up on his offer; I traveled to Greenwich, Connecticut to visit this woman. She was a wealthy Caucasian woman, and I thought to myself, what she can possibly tell this inner city woman of Caribbean and South American descent. She has no clue what my life was like, so I began to put up defenses even before meeting her. I had to make an intentional decision to conquer areas that had been compartmentalized. Numbed by life's Novocain, I didn't know how to feel again. To top it off we had to deal with grief, mourning, and to process all types of losses in our lives. I thought over time that grief and mourning only occurred when a person dies. I was so naive to the fact that I was not given proper teaching on how to go through the various stages of grief. Loss can come in the form of a relationship, death of a child, a failed business, financial support, a home, a dream, health, time, career opportunity, or anything that was significant to you as a person. There are some cultures and societies, that processing loss can be challenging. There may not be sufficient time to heal from the loss because life goes on and your responsibilities take priority and demand your attention. These variables become intertwined in the area of emotional health.

How do we grieve or mourn? I had to learn this particular skill while in this class. I could no longer hide; I had to make a conscious effort to get better. I chose to schedule my appointment with this woman. She sent me a questionnaire of probing questions, and I could feel the resistance rise within me. There was a fee, but if you want to invest in something or someone it is best to invest in 'YOU'. As I drove to meet her, the whole drive was serene and inviting. It was as if God was literally on the compounds and I parked my car and sat there for or a moment. I was not sure what to expect, but as time came near and I was walking into the quarters, she greeted me at the door. This woman was the most peaceful and free spirited person with bright blue eyes and blond hair of medium stature. She introduced herself and as I sat in the prayer room where she met with clients. She already spoke with my professor before my arrival, so she knew what I needed in this session. My deliverance and freedom from shame and guilt had to go. I would not initiate the conversation and I was very short with my answers. She began to pray and said, "Come Lord, Come Holy Spirit." She stated that if I were not going to talk then she said "we would wait". In less than a minute, which seemed like an eternity, she asked me what happened at the age of six. I thought nothing at first, but then it dawned on me that I was raised in a single family home with my mother. During that time, there was a man in my childhood pictures up until my 6th year old birthday. There was chatter that he was upset, and that I was not his child. Instantly, he rejected me because I was the child of someone else. At that vivid moment, I had made a vow in my heart that I will never let any man reject me and make me feel discarded because they were coward to love me. My heart had undergone the trauma of a lack of love, and this was the root to the many deficits growing up into a woman. The vow I made at such a young age caused me the lack of courage to ever fall in love. I had associated emotional connections to material possessions and that I was not designed for heartbreak. Once a man, started fostering any real feelings for me, I would find a fault and break it off. I did not want them to see any vulnerability, as that was a sign of weakness in my opinion. I thought no one needed to get close to me. The truth was I had become a prisoner to my rejections and shames that were placed on me from such a very young age. Even the rejection I felt from my mother played a part in all I went through.

One trauma can cause a person to falter in multiple areas, and sitting across from the therapist, I felt the pure love of Christ in the way she spoke to me. She spoke from a place of love, care and true compassion. She was the weapon used to slaughter the plans of the enemy that kept me in the coffin. Tracing back to my initial encounter with Molech, it was not on the abortion table but in the womb of my mother, when her father rejected me and her. That is where her shame started, and the cycle of having a child out of wedlock began. So much was healed and revealed during my many sessions, but it was the initial session that led me out of her doors and into my car crying. For over an hour, I sat on the highway shoulder and I cried about all the shame I ever felt, and the pains caused by a lack of knowledge and understanding. That time on the shoulder with my emergency lights flashing, was a needed encounter for me to say my shame is over! Shame no longer had its foothold in my life, and admittedly came to terms with the little girl who was fractured and healed and restored as a woman. I felt like the most blessed person as I could feel the healing balm of God flow to me.

Inner healing and soul care was a pivotal part of my new profound journey. It allowed me to dig deeper, as to why there were so many wounded persons out there. I remember hearing about an author who had conferences on emotional healing. Her name was Leanne Payne, a Pastoral Care Counselor who died at the age of 82. Her ministry and legacy was phenomenal as she ministered to many people from all walks of life. She specialized in shame, rejection and those who had been wrestling with identity issues, as well as those from depraved situations in their lives. Her material was so enriching and life altering, but hard to find. My spiritual formation was enhanced the day I heard the root cause of my problems. That was the day they were exposed and needed attention. I was on the journey to revival, and confronting all the things that had been sealed for some time. There are so many ways to know and identify the areas of shame, guilt, and rejection. Understanding the difference between each is the first step.

Shame- *a painful feeling of humiliation or distress caused by the consciousness of wrong or foolish behavior; humiliation, mortification, chagrin, ignominy, embarrassment, indignity and discomfort.*

Guilt- *a feeling of having done wrong or failed in an obligation, self-condemnation, self-reproach and shame.*

Rejection- *to refuse to accept, consider, submit to, take for some purpose, or use, to refuse to hear, receive, or admit, to rebuff, obsolete, to cast off, throw back, repulse and to spew out.*

Emotional wounds have many areas that deal with the infrastructure of a person. There are many areas to address, when dealing with your pain and the ability to heal from the pain. Freedom is a choice and it is a calculated decision to want to be free. People, who are not free, want you to be placed and remain in their bondage. If not careful, you will be enslaved and so far removed from who you were created to be. You have the ability to dealing and confront the matters of your heart, shame, guilt, rejection and emotional deprivation. There is a plethora of material and scripture verses to verbally confess over your life. Begin to examine your life in a greater way, and take the first step in getting to know who you are deep down inside. Identify the root cause of your problem, and then spend time with God and those that are objective and who can help you. These are people who will have the law of kindness in their hearts for you. It is critical to be in a safe and healthy environment, so that you can process all that you need for total deliverance. There is always a price to pay for deliverance, and the price is 'YOU'.

The word of God is the anecdote for life. There is a prescription for life within its pages. In pursuit of being free, I had to search and confess the scriptures daily. The word of God is quick and sharper than any two edged sword. It cuts, brings healing and makes us whole. There is life in the Word of God. The scriptures listed below, can help you on your journey. It is the Word of God that lasts!!

Even now, confess these scriptures daily and aloud, meditate on these verses and begin to see the love of the Father envelope you[1].

1 John 1:9 ESV- *If we confess our sins, he is faithful and just to forgive us our sins and to cleanse us from all unrighteousness.*

Isaiah 54:4 ESV - *Fear not, for you will not be ashamed; be not confounded, for you will not be disgraced; for you will forget the shame of your youth, and the reproach of your widowhood you will remember no more.*

Revelation 21:4 ESV- *He will wipe away every tear from their eyes, and death shall be no more, neither shall there be mourning, nor crying, nor pain anymore, for the former things have passed away.*

---

[1] www.openbible.info/topics/guilt_and_shame

Romans 3:23 ESV- *For all have sinned and fall short of the glory of God,*

Acts 8:22 ESV- *Repent, therefore, of this wickedness of yours, and pray to the Lord that, if possible, the intent of your heart may be forgiven you.*

Micah 7:19 ESV- *He will again have compassion on us; he will tread our iniquities underfoot. You will cast all our sins into the depths of the sea.*

Acts 3:19 ESV- *Repent therefore, and turn again, that your sins may be blotted out,*

Psalm 103:8-12 ESV- *The LORD is merciful and gracious, slow to anger and abounding in steadfast love. He will not always chide, nor will he keep his anger forever. He does not deal with us according to our sins, nor repay us according to our iniquities. For as high as the heavens are above the earth, so great is his steadfast love toward those who fear him; as far as the east is from the west, so far does he remove our transgressions from us.*

Philippians 4:13 ESV - *I can do all things through him who strengthens me.*

Hebrews 10:15-18 ESV- *And the Holy Spirit also bears witness to us; for after saying, "This is the covenant that I will make with them after those days, declares the Lord: I will put my laws on their hearts, and write them on their minds," then he adds, "I will remember their sins and their lawless deeds no more." Where there is* forgiveness of these, there is no longer any offering for sin.

1 John 2:2 ESV- *He is the propitiation for our sins, and not for ours only but also for the sins of the whole world.*

Romans 10:9 ESV- *Because, if you confess with your mouth that Jesus is Lord and believe in your heart that God raised him from the dead, you will be saved.*

John 3:18 ESV- *Whoever believes in him is not condemned, but whoever does not believe is condemned already, because he has not believed in the name of the only Son of God.*

Isaiah 50:7 ESV- *But the Lord GOD helps me; therefore I have not been disgraced; therefore I have set my face like a flint, and I know that I shall not be put to shame.*

Acts 2:38 ESV- *And Peter said to them, "Repent and be baptized every one of you in the name of Jesus Christ for the forgiveness of your sins, and you will receive the gift of the Holy Spirit.*

Psalm 103:1-22 ESV- *Of David. Bless the LORD, O my soul, and all that is within me, bless his holy name! Bless the LORD, O my soul, and forget not all his benefits, who forgives all your iniquity, who heals all your diseases, who redeems your life from the pit, who crowns you with steadfast love and mercy, who satisfies you with good so that your youth is renewed like the eagle's.*

1 Timothy 2:4 ESV- *Who desires all people to be saved and to come to the knowledge of the truth.*

Psalm 22:5 ESV- *To you they cried and were rescued; in you they trusted and were not put to shame.*

Romans 8:28 ESV- *And we know that for those who love God all things work together for good, for those who are called according to his purpose.*

Psalm 34:5 ESV- *Those who look to him are radiant, and their faces shall never be ashamed.*

Hebrews 12:2 ESV- *Looking to Jesus, the founder and perfecter of our faith, who for the joy that was set before him endured the cross, despising the shame, and is seated at the right hand of the throne of God.*

John 5:24 ESV- *Truly, truly, I say to you, whoever hears my word and believes him who sent me has eternal life. He does not come into judgment, but has passed from death to life.*

John 3:15 ESV- *That whoever believes in him may have eternal life.*

2 Peter 2:9 ESV- *Then the Lord knows how to rescue the godly from trials, and to keep the unrighteous under punishment until the day of judgment.*

James 5:16 ESV- *Therefore, confess your sins to one another and pray for one another, that you may be* *healed. The prayer of a righteous person has great power as it is working.*

Romans 1:16 ESV- *For I am not ashamed of the gospel, for it is the power of God for salvation to everyone who believes, to the Jew first and also to the Greek.*

Rejoice you have allowed the Spirit of God to meet you at your first step. Your shame, guilt, fears, and pain has been forgiven. He loves you and your sin and shame has been placed in the sea of forgetfulness. You are free to go, free to live on purpose, free to live a liberated life because who the Son sets free, is free indeed.

Chapter 9

You will be a sacrifice, 2018

As the years went on, there was much to do, and many deadlines to meet. While working in ministry, I came to a standstill and decided it was best to stop my lengthy itinerary. There was much on my plate, including the writing of this manuscript. In 2002, I was instructed to write a book on shame, and the effects of what the enemy had done throughout my life.

The enemy is real! However, Gods power is greater! The writing of this book has been an uphill trek from the beginning. There was much apprehension in wanting to share my story. The truth is, a part of me wanted my secrets to be hidden. Talking about the details of my life, meant welcoming comments and opinions from people. When attending churches, I developed a discipline, never to get close to any of the congregants or the leadership. In my mind, if I was not on an assignment, the less engagement, the better for me. For many years, I would go in and out of the church, not saying much to people, and leaving as soon as the benediction was pronounced. I was free of drama, and people who with their jealousy and envy of me. This was my preference; to not have people know anything about me.

Eventually, there came a time during many transitions in my life that I decided to partner with a particular ministry. I wanted to sit under a ministry, that I could receive the word of God. My life seemed to be stripping me of all comforts. My movement, if not God ordained, was few and far off of the radar. Over the years, God had only released me from the protection in his wings to minister and go on assignments, and when I was done, he would bring me back into himself. This is how God continually protected me. Many people viewed me with jaded and critical eyes and were unfriendly. Casting their judgments and the look of snare was normal as they only saw the outside appearance and had no interest in the actual person within. There was more beyond the makeup, smile, eyes, and clothing. Many people would try to get to know me but then treated me indifferent because of their insecurities. Along with this journey, I saw the good in people and wanted to know, how a person can be jealous towards others who are suffering and in pain. I often wondered, why some call themselves 'Christians' while being toxic to others and coveting another persons' testimony and blessings? It's as if there is a comparison of the depth of suffering each person has undergone in relation to the anointing on their life. Each person has their portion of shaming, disappointment, betrayal, pain, and deprivations. Much takes place during the reigns of our mind, heart, emotions, and daily life. What is most surprising, is many people worship and attend services, and go home feeling alone, afraid, sad, disheartened, discouraged, tormented, and gripped with fear, not able to see their way out.

While in ministry, I have counseled many on the verge of walking away from God. Some who even considered taking their own life because they put their trust in man above trusting God. Some who felt that if they are serving a loving and Triune God, why is deliverance not happening to them fast enough. There are many emotional wounds causing people to disconnect form their source, Jesus Christ. They have left the Holy Spirit out of the equation and took on the task of trying to hold their own lives together. In retrospect, I had to go back to an assessment taken a while back. It was a personality test of 16 different traits, and the one that stood out the most to me was 'self-sufficient'. This trait was a significant warning sign for me. If I am not careful in the way I make choices and dealing with people, and I would end up getting in trouble with God. I was too self-sufficient and didn't feel the need for anyone to do what I could do for myself. So many times I pretended like I was okay, but deep down I was desensitized from receiving the authentic touch and deliverance of God. How can we ask to be free, without being honest with ourselves? If we tell ourselves we are okay, and are not, then we are lying to the person in the mirror. The Word of God is a mirror. Standing in front of a physical mirror, I remember seeing a horrid sight looking back. In a vision, there was a smokescreen, and I was could see the sinfulness of sin. It was as if all the bad things and distasteful choices I made were looking back at me as I confronted each thing. The Bible tells us that the truth will set us free, but you and I both have allowed the enemy to speak to our minds that we are well and functioning in our maximum ability, but it is a false self. The false self always wants to parade and be the one that stays on the surface, while the real person is under all the camouflage. The endless self-talk that talks us out of what God is saying to us and makes us negate from our real purpose. We have managed to be like a chameleon changing and adapting to our environment, even to the point where there is no authenticity. In my perspective, my authenticity is real because I only know myself. I cannot place myself in the place of God. It is a dangerous position when we muster up the confidence to play the role of God. It is dangerous to feel we can control, create, and foster things that only God can. Over and over again, I learned that the false self is a representative that only last for a short while. The real self will still appear and present itself at any given moment. I made the decision a long time ago that I would always be my real self, and true deliverance is a choice! I would no longer be enslaved to hiding things from the past. I have to make a conscious effort to put down the aura and persona of who I perceived myself to be and let God reveal to me who I am to Him. When God tells you that you will be set free, he does not wait for a day or months, or years. When you are set free by God, it's instantaneous. There were so many blessings released my way in the past because of false self. However, it caused me to miss out on significant breakthroughs, which led to walking around the mountain of disobedience and defeat. I did not have the emotional and physical stamina to repeat certain cycles, so many strongholds had to be made low and crushed.

In 2018, I could feel an urgency to be intentional in everything I would do. It was a time and journey that I had to do alone. There was no room for self-pity, and I could not have people around me as a crutch. This was a time where fewer people would have access to my life. Minimal guiding and minimal people could hear my heart, so I was processing in silence. Processing being misunderstood, processing why am I in this particular place, and what is the purpose behind all this transitioning. There were many plaguing questions in my mind. Then it dawned on me; there is another level of acceleration and alignment needed for this new phase of my life. This was a new place that I never saw before in my life, a place that was unknown. It was an incubator, life and death place. I was in a gestational period hoping and praying this lonely obsolete place would come to an end. Why am I feeling like this? Why am I experiencing all this pain, but in actuality everything hurts and is contrary to the many words prophesied over my life? Who is Nabiha and why does it seem as if she is losing every area of comfort? When God is moving you by force, there is not much talking. He will guide you better than you can guide yourself. God whispered to me, "It is time to confront and deal with Molech for my hand is here to deliver thee."

Molech your assignment is up!!!

The Bible tells us that Ruth had a Naomi, Esther had a Mordecai, Elizabeth had a Mary, Lazarus had Jesus and mankind had Jesus. Jesus died, resurrected and ascended on high and sits at the right hand of the Father in Heaven. Every person on the road to destiny needs a person in the form of a midwife, kinsman redeemer, and encourager. Someone to chastise them, correct and edifies to bring forth the greatness within. It is a time to trust those around you who can speak into your life and speak objectively. There is safety in the midst of counsel. When in transition or making great decisions, seeking the Lord is very imperative. Leaning on God wholeheartedly is a major key to getting to your destination. You have to trust God even when it hurts. There won't be any cheerleaders on the sidelines telling you that you are on the right path. All you have at that moment is blind faith. You have to amplify your trust in God, and believe that he makes all things beautiful in His time. Surely, this moment in time-tested me to the core. It tested if I was hearing from God without God speaking to me at all. It was a knowing and listening to the guide of the Holy Spirit. On different occasions, he would send a Prophet or Prophetess to speak into my life. They would provide clarification that I was on the right path. God was honoring my faithfulness and my obedience in a time what seemed dismal and barren. Even I needed the reassurance that God was going to keep and lead me to the peaceful shore. God never failed me and being in the middle of the ocean, there were two options, sink or swim. I chose to obey God, and not disappoint Him as I did in the past. I questioned, cried, got frustrated and cumbersome, but his peace remained steady in my life. God can do just what he said He would do. God perfects all that concerns both you and me. God is a promise keeper. God is the deliverer that lifts downtrodden heads out of the dung places. If I could describe the feeling I was having, it felt as if I was in a deep precipice, hanging over into a high hazardous place. All of my comforts and resources were dangling before my eyes, and God began to cut away so many things in my life. "Trust me, you can't go further without trusting me," God said. I thought I did trust God until I was faced with a greater level and depth of vulnerability. My expectation level had to be high in 2018, as there was much loss and testing exiting 2017. I made a major life-altering decision that year. If I was honestly going to meet God more profoundly, a lot of things needed to be defied and confronted. What more did I have to confront? Is there more Lord? Absolutely! I sought the face of God, and the Holy Spirit assured me that in time I would see.

In January 2018, I was supposed to travel overseas and decided to cancel and attend a retreat titled 'Greater Depth'. There was such a pulling and need to be on this retreat that I did not want to miss it. I attended as a guest, but something inside me was brewing. Sometimes the Lord will use me at the spur of the moment, even when I am not the assigned speaker. I follow the Holy Spirit's unction and obey when he gives me something to say or do. On January 13, 2018, a pastor was preaching, and at the close of the session, he ministered to me. With such precision, he spoke into my life and said, "The gestation period is over. This place in your prayer chamber will give you strategy, for you have a master business mind and are a woman who seeks God face to face."

Little did he know, I was hiding in the cleft of the rock seeking God and constantly talking to him about my purpose and his people. While praying, I believed God for everyone else but forgot to pray and intercede for myself. I began to scan the room, and I got a heavy burden for every person that was in attendance. Praying earnestly, I asked the Lord to give us a divine visitation before the close of the conference. Later on that day, I went back to my room to settled in and prepare for Morning Prayer in the sanctuary. There was uneasiness in my spirit, and as I laid in the bed tears began to fill my eyes. I was crying uncontrollably, and could not stop. It was as if God entered my room. I began confessing, "Something has to die." I wondered if God heard my cry. I was in a place of loneliness, and away from all the distractions. It was a time where I needed God to show me who He is and why I was on this particular retreat.

On January 14, 2018, at 4:38 AM, my eyes opened as still in the bed. It came to me, the number fourteen, and the number of deliverance and today was my day. "Today is the day, you will be a sacrifice," God said to me.

During the Morning Prayer session, and through the remainder of the day, I pondered what that meant. I was relieved that the pastor did not call me to preach or teach, I was just there to receive whatever God wanted to do. About 2:00 PM, we were gathered in the sanctuary, for the next session titled 'Beneath the makeup'. The description in the bulletin read: Describe your scars and share a beautiful testimony that you have made it. Life has thrown all it can at you, and you are still standing amongst more. Reading the caption, I did not know what to expect. A dear woman of God asked a few women to assist her. She began to tell her story with us and described the testing she went through during her life. Her testimony opened the floor for others to step up and share their own. A young lady began to share her story and then paused, as she was struggling to get her words out. A woman and I went over to help. We began to renounce and denounce certain things, and then confess positive declarations for her deliverance. Afterward, she finished up her testimony, and as I stood near her, I could feel the Spirit of the Lord nudging me to tell my story. I tried to avoid the prompting and just watched other women come forth with their testimonies. Then the pastor came into the room and sat down in the back. I thought to myself, if I were going to share, I would wait for him to leave the room. As each woman spoke and shared their story, deliverance filled the room. It was a critical time for me to stop wrestling and fighting against sharing my story. As soon as the session was closing, the Holy Spirit said, "Tell your story now, the bait is ripe, and deliverance shall be wrought. You have to be comfortable sharing your story with others because the book you are writing will save many and free those who are enslaved to shame and rejection." I was so afraid and ashamed to open my mouth, but I was more fearful of not obeying God in front of all these women and now a man in the room.

At that moment, I felt fear, because I did not know what would happen. Who would love me after this? A powerful range of emotions flooded my heart, and nervousness and battle raged in my mind that should keep my mouth closed. As I spoke, it took me back to the first time I laid on the abortion table. I began to smell the medicine, the fire, the burning corpse of the babies; I saw the address 44 Court Street, Brooklyn, NY and flashes of the god of Molech. I kept my eyes closed because I did not want to see anyone's face looking back at me. "I was a seven-time felon," I said. At that moment, many people did not understand what I meant. I was on death row for being a murderer, performing a child sacrifice. As I told my story, I could hear the cries of the women and deliverance hitting the whole room. My eyes were filled with tears, to the point where I wanted this day to be over and run to my room. I remember after I spoke, it was addressed that I needed the walls to come down, but the demon of being defensive tried to suck me back into that place of my grave situation. As the pastor ministered to me, I leaned over the table, and it felt like I was sewn back up. The tenderness and love of the heavenly Father were flowing through the pastor. I no longer was carrying the broken, discarded young girl who had many depths of pain. That young girl from long ago no longer dwelled in the valley of the dead or participated in the murderous acts of children condoned by the government. The cycle of abortion was over, and for the first time, my shame was not judged. It was a moment of reconciliation for me and others, who were in need of a father's love and affection. God's timing is always strategic. This deliverance session was a pivotal point in my life. It was the last part before I could conclude the writing of this book. I thought what man would want to love me knowing all of my treacherous past? Several women embraced me and started calling out numbers of their felonies. Knowing that sharing my story helped so many women get their deliverance meant so much to me. Standing in the gap, and being bold and courageous was not the easiest thing to do but it was necessary so that God would receive all Glory. My deliverance was, is and continues to be real. I have accepted all things in this process of deliverance. All of my disappointments and setbacks ended when I decided to confront my truth and own deliverance. Free from condemnation, ridicule, and all negative comments said, or that may be asserted against me after the release of this book. I am God's redemptive work. Deliverance is a choice, and it is available for you today!

It was a moment for me to know that being that sacrifice was necessary. Even now as I write, my tears are flowing because God is always intentional. He has never cast me away but continues to give me the opportune time to tell my story to a depraved nation. To share with those who need liberty from the spirit of shame and rejection. To be set free from the place of Tophet. In the Hebrew Bible, the prophet Jeremiah talks about the high places of Topheth. Topheth also referred to as Tophet was a location in Jerusalem in the Gehinnom, where worshippers were influenced by the ancient Canaanite religion and engaged in the human sacrifice of children to the gods Moloch, Molech, and Baal. They would burn these children alive. Later on, Tophet would become a theological or poetic synonym for hell within Christendom. I can say the day of my deliverance came as a mighty rushing wind to free my soul from sin and death. I come as a Prophet, the mouthpiece of God for each person reading this book. If you are a woman or a man, your shame, infirmity, rejection, and pain have been redeemed when Jesus set all captivity free. You and I have a voice of the King that rules and reigns within. This day harden not your heart, for healing is flowing your way. Just pray these simple words, "Father, I need your healing power to dissolve every pain and every residue away." He is a Father who is always in touch with our infirmities. He is a Father who loves us even when we feel damaged, used and abused. He is a loving Father who has preserved your life for such a time as this.

There are so many tools to help us identify whether the emotional wounds have been dealt with from our past. We can utilize resources that are available while learning and growing from those who can give you wise counsel along your journey to recovery. I will say that I do not look like my past. There is victory after the battle! You can overcome any obstacles the enemy may throw your way. God is gracious, and he has given this particular assignment to me because I am a true essence of his handiwork, yet I am still on the Potter's Wheel. His love is from everlasting to everlasting, and his strength is made perfect in our weaknesses. He is the lifter of our head and a way maker who is not partial. What he continues to do for me, He promised to do for all those who call on the name of the Lord. He is our Rock and Strong Tower and never loses a battle, undefeated in every arena. As you magnify God, the Lord Jesus Christ is faithful and just to visit you. Call on the name of the Lord while He may be found. He is a rewarder to those that diligently seek him. Have faith, only believe that He formed and chose you before the foundation of the world and each one of you was on his mind. Our Father in Heaven is gracious, and his Grace is Sufficient. In all things give thanks, and watch God meet you at the point of your need. In the Bible, the children of Israel recovered all, and you too SHALL RECOVER ALL!!

YOU NO LONGER ARE IMPRISONED TO THE GOD OF SHAME, THE SPIRIT OF MURDER, SHAME, and REJECTION HAS BEEN DEFEATED ON THE CROSS!!

THE BLOOD OF JESUS CHRIST HAS REDEEMED YOU!! REJOICE

Molech has been broken!

About the Author

Nabiha Kelly is a prolific woman of God who has embarked the call of ministry at a delicate age. As the founder of Nabiha Kelly Ministries International she labors in the vineyard for the Kingdom of God to be advanced, and mother of two with a vast amount of spiritual children divinely given. She is a native born and raised in Brooklyn, NY of dissent from Guyana in South America, she attended and excelled in the New York City Public school system, and then went on to complete her Bachelor of Arts at John Jay College of Criminal Justice. In 2005, it was prophetically spoken that it was time for Nabiha to pursue higher education in religious studies. The Bible tells us to study to show thyself approved and in 2012 Nabiha made a huge pivotal step and graduated with a degree in Master of Divinity from Nyack College-Alliance Theological Seminary. She is currently pursuing her Doctorate of Ministry in Global Leadership at Nyack College-Alliance Theological Seminary.

Nabiha has been one who is called to bombard the gates of hell and to back up every contrary force that will come in the way of Gods Will through intercession, ministering the

Word of God around the world, accurate prophetic "a now word", and her extraordinary ability to proclaim the Good News to all she encounters with power, authority and confidence. With heart and passion for the things of God it is a crucial element that her heart's desire is to see blind eyes open, the lame to walk, the opening of prison doors, cast out devils, and heal all that are oppressed and the captives to be set free and for all to know Jesus face to face and not through religion. Jesus Christ is real and her famous quote is "God is on the throne". Jesus commissioned us to be disciples and to do greater works in His Name. Many can describe Nabiha as one who has a "ducks back", as she has the tenacity and vigor to overcome any obstacle faced while shaking all the things off that comes at her. Through much suffering and reigning with God the process of the "Call" has been eminent to those who are in her presence. She is transparent and bold and is shy of being timid when it comes to confronting ones destiny.

With uncompromising faith and being knocked down but not destroyed Nabiha has always been able by God's strength and power to always stand in the midst of the fire and not look or smell burnt. She is a woman who has experienced so many trials, triumphs and the continual process of being on the Potter's Wheel. With great zeal to see the miraculous work of God through the work of the Son Jesus Christ our Savior be manifested here on earth. Nabiha has been proved and is still proven to be one who will stand when all odds are against her.

Through much "church" hurt, pain, despair and a vivid tainted past Nabiha is a clear distinction that God's grace, favor, love, power, and anointing is able to set free, transform, deliver and catapult one for His use and is able to transcend all opposition of the nay says.

As a trailblazer and much sought after preacher it is with great admonishing that Nabiha is the ideal runner in this race and has been called to captivate any audience when she steps in the room with the evident anointing that is second to none given by the Gift Giver. She truly has a tailor made calling from the Master that can't be reproduced as she is considered to be someone compared to tapestry, a beautiful fabric that has been interwoven over and over again which creates an awesome pattern.

Made in the USA
Lexington, KY
11 November 2019

56847630R00085